T0363838

MORE! 2nd Edition 4

Herbert Puchta & Jeff Stranks
G. Gerngross C. Holzmann P. Lewis-Jones

HELBLING LANGUAGES

Workbook

CAMBRIDGE UNIVERSITY PRESS
www.cambridge.org/elt

HELBLING LANGUAGES
www.helblinglanguages.com

MORE! 2nd Edition Workbook 4
by Herbert Puchta & Jeff Stranks with G. Gerngross, C. Holzmann, P. Lewis Jones

© Cambridge **University Press and Helbling Languages 2014**
(*More* was originally published by Helbling Languages © Helbling Languages 2006)

First published 2014
20 19 18 17 16 15 14 13 12 11

Printed in Malaysia by Vivar Printing

A catalogue record for this book is available from the British Library

ISBN 9781 107640511 MORE! 2nd Edition Student's Book 4
ISBN 9781 107652941 MORE! 2nd Edition Workbook 4
ISBN 9781 107682993 MORE! 2nd Edition Teacher's Book 4
ISBN 9781 107669826 MORE! 2nd Edition Audio Set 4 (3 CDs)
ISBN 9781 107643314 MORE! 2nd Edition Testbuilder CD-ROM 4
ISBN 9781 107654020 MORE! 2nd Edition Presentation Plus DVD-ROM Level 4
ISBN 9781 107666276 MORE! 2nd Edition *School Reporters* DVD 4

The authors would like to thank:
Oonagh Wade and Rosamund Cantalamessa for their expertise in working on the manuscripts, their useful suggestions for improvement, and the support we got from them.

Lucia Astuti and Markus Spielmann, Helbling Languages, Frances Lowndes and James Dingle, Cambridge University Press, for their dedication to the project and innovative publishing vision.

Our designers, Amanda Hockin, Richard Jervis and the team at Pixarte. Also, our art editors, Francesca Gironi and Veronica Stecconi for their dedicated work.

The publishers would like to thank the following for their kind permission to reproduce the following photographs and other copyright material:

©Web Pix p9 (Youtube.com Felix Baumgartner Red Bull jump website screenshot), Grapheast p52 (Arab greeting), Pictorial Press Ltd p61 (Frozen; Gravity) **/Alamy; Bradley Ambrose** p10 (Geoff Mackley); Rui Matos p13, Guido Amrein p14 (Antarctica), Ron Sumners p15 (Uluru), Derek Rogers p15 (Antarctica), Indos82 p15 (map of Antarctica), Andrzej Tokarski p17 (umbrella), Alexander Pladdet p17 (torch), Nicku p18 (girl on the left), Photomak p21 , Elena Elisseeva p22, Tomáš Prokop p24 (Jenny), Leslie Banks p24 (David), Galina Barskaya p26, Brad Calkins p27 (Taj Mahal), Ekaterina Pokrovsky p28 (father and son), Juliengrondin p28 (Asian woman), Ljupco Smokovski p29 (teenage boy), DM7 p29 (artwork), Iakov Filimonov p36, Kierran Allen p38 (Moses Mabhida Stadium World Cup), Aguina p38 (Brazil World Cup trophy), Bjørn Hovdal p40, Czuber p42 (man), Mastroraf p42 (Game of Chess in Marostica), Luciano Mortula p43 (Venice Carnival), Sabrina Cercelovic p47 (fried egg and bread), Monkey Business Images p51 (mother and baby), sturti p60, Hodzha p61 (Cds), Bartlomiej Magierowski p64 (Lara), Meaothai p66 (Harley Davinson), Ivan Cholakov p66 (jet airplane), Klikin p66 (Banksy), Vlights p67 (boy playing guitar), Douglas Raphael p71 (stamp collection), Alextara p84 (Lindi), John Wollwerth p84 (Koli), Photographerlondon p85, William Berry p86 I**Dreamstime.com;** © Daniel Ernst - **Fotolia.com** p32; ©iStockphoto.com/ bmcent1 p4 (teenagers cooking), Bikeworldtravel p11, bluecinema p23, dimdimich p29 (hourglass), Ridofranz p31 (boy no. 2), tunart p52 (Japanese greeting), helovi p52 (women kissing), Opla p56, wetcake p67 (girl playing piano), theboone p67 (woman gardening), EdStock p80; **NASA** p16 (Tristan da Cunha Island, South Atlantic Ocean); Africa Studio p4 (teenagers studying), Syda Productions p4 (teenagers watching tv), Byelikova Oksana p14 (Papua New Guinea), bierchen p14 (angler fish), Pi-Lens p15 (greenhouse), Alexey Boldin p17 (smartphone), gcpics p17 (chocolate), forest badger p17 (boots), Mega Pixel p17 (First Aid Kit Box), Samuel Borges Photography p24 (Maria), aldegonde p24 (Paul), aastock p24 (Olivia), Luciano Mortula p27 (The Statue of Liberty), Ammentorp Photography p28 (Theo Manatos), Peter Bernik p28 (businesswoman with tablet), Nejron Photo p29 (elderly care specialist), Kritchanut p29 (vertical garden), Marko Marcello p30, AlenD p31 (boy no. 1), Daniel M Ernst p31 (girl no. 3), PT Images p31 (boy no. 4), T-Design p31 (girl no. 5), leedsn p31 (girl no. 6), Bule Sky Studio p42 (Ayuttaya, Thailand), M. Rohana p43 (Palio, Siena), Paolo Bona p43 (Carnival, Ivrea), Olesya Feketa p44, Monkey Business Images p45, Alex459 p47 (chocolate cake), Shahril KHMD p51 (chocolate), l i g h t p o e t p51 (woman running), monticello p51 (fruit), kurhan p51 (smile), S.Tiptanatoranin p52 (Thai women), wong yu liang p52 (Chinese greeting), Tyler Olson p59 (photo A), EDHAR p59 (agreement), cinemafestival p61 (Leonardo di Caprio), s_bukley p61 (Bruno Mars), Featureflash p61 (Jesse J.), DFree p61 (Sandra Bullock), JStone p61 (One Direction), Samuel Borges Photography p62, Max Topchii p64 (Alison), MJTH p64 (Jonathan), spinetta p66 (typewriter), luca85 p66, ifong p67 (girl with laptop), Eziutka p70 (photo no. 1), photka p70 (photo no. 2), SNEHIT p71 (dolls collection), photopixel p71 (cds), Meg Wallace Photography p72, aGinger p73, Helder Almeida p74, p79, pavalena p84 (map), Jeanette Dietl p84 (Kwame), baranq p87 **/Shutterstock.com**.

Illustrated by Michele Farella, Giovanni Giorgi Pierfranceschi, Mirella Mariani, Laura Desirée Pozzi.

Every effort has been made to trace the owners of any copyright material in this book. If notified, the publishers will be pleased to rectify any errors or omissions.

Contents

Dialogue work

1 Complete the dialogue with the correct form of the verbs in brackets. Then listen and check.

Jesse Hi, Emma!

Emma Hi! Sorry, I'm late. Wow, what are all these people [1] .... (do) here today?

Jesse We're near Wembley stadium, remember! There's a football match on. It's funny, I've [2] .... (live) here since I was born but I've never been to the stadium before. Have you ever been to a football match?

Emma Yes, I've [3] .... (be) to a few matches. At school! Hey, look at that guy over there. I think he's lost … Hello! Are you [4] .... (look) for the stadium?

Zach Oh, hi. Yes, I am!

Jesse It's very near here. Just walk straight up here and then turn right at the end of the street. Where are you from?

Zach I'm from the States. I'm [5] .... (study) here in London.

Emma How long have you been here?

Zach For two weeks. I've always [6] .... (want) to see an English soccer game … But I haven't got a ticket. Have you [7] .... (buy) tickets?

Jesse No, we aren't [8] .... (go) to the match. We're going to have a coffee! Would you [9] .... (like) to come? There's a good place just near here.

Zach OK! Great!

2 Complete the sentences.

1 Emma says 'sorry' because ....

2 There are lots of people today because ....

3 Jesse has lived in Wembley ....

4 Zach lives ....

5 He's in the UK because ....

3 Listen to the dialogues. Match the people and the activities.

1	Suzy is	a	studying
2	Mark is	b	watching TV
3	Annie is	c	cooking
4	Jack is		

Vocabulary and Communication

Sports and sports clothes

1 Reorder the letters below and write the words in the correct box.

obsto   volegs   slegogg   methel   daps   hstir   thorss   skocs   stariner   stev

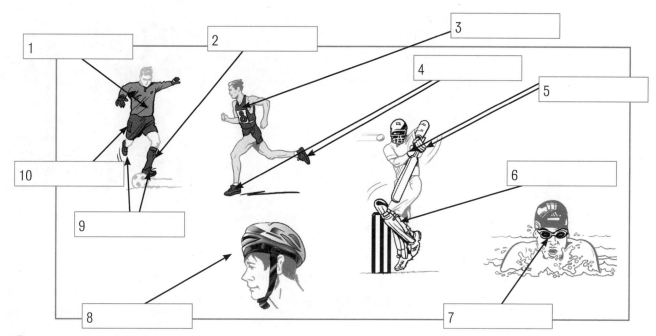

2 Complete the phrases with the words from exercise 1.

1 a football   *shirt*.................
2 a pair of   ....
3 a running   ....
4 a pair of   ....
5 a pair of   ....

6 knee   ....
7 a pair of swimming ....
8 a cycling   ....
9 a pair of football ....
10 a pair of   ....

Buying things in a sports shop

04
CD1

3 Complete the dialogue with the words below. Then listen and check.

pair   try   help   size

ⓖ- sport

Assistant Can I ¹ .... you?
Customer Yes, I need a ² .... of cycling shorts.
Assistant OK. What ³ .... are you?
Customer Eight, I think.
Assistant OK. Would you like to ⁴ .... these on?
Customer Thanks.

05
CD1

4 # Sounds right /s/ vs. /z/ in plural nouns

Listen and circle the /s/ sounds and underline the /z/ sounds.

1 sports   2 clothes   3 cycling shorts   4 trainers

Grammar

Present simple, Present continuous, Present perfect

1 Read the sentences. Write Present simple (PS), Present continuous (PC), or Present perfect (PP) after each one.

1 Look – she's running really quickly. ....PC........
2 I'm watching a match on TV right now. ....
3 I haven't moved for the last two hours! ....
4 What are you doing? ....
5 I go to the gym three times a week. ....
6 I'm making some food. ....
7 I've never played cricket. ....
8 I don't play any sports – I'm too lazy! ....
9 I watch football every weekend. ....
10 I've just watched a great film! ....

2 Match the forms to their uses.

1 Present simple   a talk about experiences
2 Present continuous   b habits and routines
3 Present perfect   c things happening now

3 Circle the correct verbs.

1 At the moment, *I'm training / I train* for a marathon. It's really hard!
2 You *are having / have had* these football boots for two years – why don't you buy a new pair?
3 She *doesn't like / isn't liking* tennis – she prefers volleyball.
4 *I've never played / I am not playing* rugby – what's it like?
5 Mark is in front of the TV – *he watches / he's watching* a football match.
6 I *have wanted / want* to buy a new pair of shoes – these ones are really old.
7 *I've worn / I'm wearing* gloves because my hands are cold.
8 He always *wears / is wearing* a helmet when he goes cycling.

4 Complete the sentences with the Present perfect form of the verbs in brackets.

1 .... this football shirt for a long time. (I / have)
2 .... to a football match? (you / be)
3 She's nervous because .... a marathon before. (she / not run)
4 .... to learn to swim. (he / always want)
5 .... that new cycling helmet yet? (he / buy)
6 .... to the gym for two weeks. (I / not be)

Grammar

5 Complete the text messages with the correct form of the verbs in brackets.

A

Hi Mark. Thanks for telling me about the exam 2morrow! I'm
¹ .... (study) for it now.
Have you ² .... (finish) studying yet?

Jack

B

Hi Jack. Well, I've ³ .... (do) my Maths revision and I'm
⁴ .... (do) some English now.

Mark

C

What? We ⁵ .... (need) to study Maths, too?

Jack

D

Yes! Have you ⁶ .... (forget) that too? We've got Maths and English 2morrow.

Mark

E

What??! OK. I ⁷ .... (not think) I'll get much sleep tonight ...

Jack

F

Don't worry! I've just ⁸ .... (text) Suzy and Ann. They haven't
⁹ .... (study) for Maths either!

Mark

6 Complete the questions and answers with the correct form of the Present perfect tense.

1 Has Jack ...*revised*... (revise) for his Maths and English exams? No, he ....
2 Has Mark .... (do) any Maths revision? Yes, he ....
3 Have Suzy and Ann .... (receive) a message from Mark? Yes, they ....
4 Have Suzy and Ann .... (study) for the Maths exams? No, they ....

7 Match the questions and answers.

1 Do you often go swimming?
2 How long have you been training?
3 Have you ever seen a football match?
4 What are you doing?
5 Do you like cricket?
6 Has he been to the gym?
7 Has your hair always been blonde?
8 What's the best thing you've ever done?
9 Are you working at the moment?

a No, I haven't.
b Yes – that's why he looks tired.
c Yes, but I prefer football.
d For two months.
e No, I'm not.
f Yes – every weekend.
g I once ran a marathon in 3 hours.
h I'm buying some clothes online.
i Yes, since I was born.

Skills

Reading

1 Look at the photo. What do you think the person is doing?

2 Read the article and answer the questions.

Would you enjoy clinging on to the vertical wall on the outside of a 90-floor office block with hundreds of people watching you from the ground – and police waiting to arrest you when you reached the top of the building?

Well, it's just a normal day in the life of Alain Robert, 'the human spider'. Alain is a world-famous French 'free urban climber'. Free climbers like Alain don't usually use any ropes, helmets or other safety equipment – they climb using just their bare hands and climbing shoes. It's one of the most dangerous sports in the world.

And Alain doesn't climb for fame or money – although he has earned money through climbing some buildings for advertising. (A few years ago, he climbed a building in London, wearing a *Spiderman* costume, to promote the new film.)

He began climbing rock cliffs as a young boy. His first 'free climb' was when he was 11 or 12. He'd forgotten his keys and couldn't get into his home on the seventh floor of a block of flats. So, instead of waiting for his parents to come home, he climbed the outside of the block of flats and got in through an open window. He says that from that moment on, he wanted to be a climber.

Since then, he has climbed more than 80 of the world's tallest buildings – usually without permission. He has been arrested several times after these climbs, and has had five serious falls in his life. But none of these experiences has stopped him from attempting more and more dangerous climbs.

He admits that he puts his life in danger every time he climbs, but he says that climbing this way has now become 'a habit'. Which building is he planning to climb next?

We'll have to wait and see!

1 How long has Alain Robert been free climbing?

....

2 How many buildings has he climbed?

....

3 Has anyone ever paid him for climbing? When? Why?

....

4 Has he ever had serious accidents?

....

5 Why do the police often arrest him after his climbs?

....

6 What building is he planning to climb next?

....

Skills

Listening

3 Look at the photo and guess the answers to the questions.

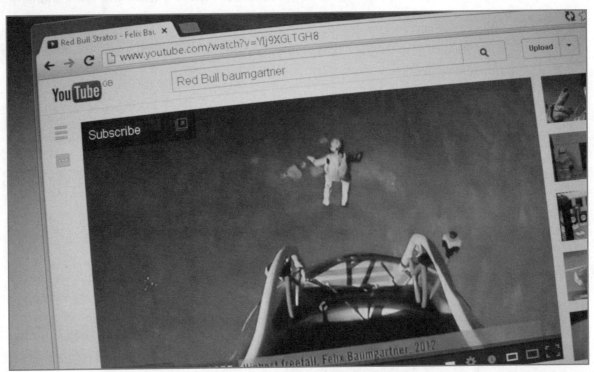

1 What is the man doing?

....

2 How high is he above the Earth?

....

3 How fast did he travel?

....

4 How long was the fall?

....

5 How many people watched him?

....

4 Listen and check your answers.

Writing

5 Plan an email to a friend about a sport. Follow the instructions.

1 Think about a sport you have done, or a sport you have seen recently.
2 Make notes about what happens. For example, was it exciting or difficult? What do you do in this sport? What do you wear? Does somebody win?
3 How do you feel about this sport? Would you like to do it or watch it again?

6 Write your email to a friend about the sport.

Text work

1 Look at the photo and the title of the article. Tick (✓) what you think the article is about.

someone who studies volcanoes ☐
someone who takes dangerous photos ☐
someone who takes photos of travellers ☐

2 Read the article and check your answer.

Geoff Mackley – extreme photographer

Have you ever thought what it would be like to stand at the top of a volcano and look inside while it's erupting?

Geoff Mackley is a photographer. He was born in New Zealand and he spent a lot of his life chasing storms across the world and taking dramatic photos.

According to Mackley, there are few places in the world today where you can stand, look around and say 'I am the only person who has ever been here.' That's why he went to Mount Marum – an active volcano on the island of Ambryn. This island, in the South Pacific near Australia, is also called the 'black island' because of its dark volcanic rock. And it is here that Mackley took some of his most dramatic photos.

As the volcano was erupting, Mackley climbed down 1,700 feet inside Mount Marum. The temperature around him was an incredible 2,000 °C but luckily he had prepared well. With a special heat-resistant suit, he was able to survive the high temperatures. Without these special clothes, a human could only stay for a few seconds near the boiling lava - Mackley managed to stay there for over 40 minutes, filming. He had also brought special oxygen tanks with him, because if he had breathed the volcanic gases, he would have died immediately.

Geoff Mackley could only stay for a fairly short time inside the volcano, but he took some fantastic photos. But perhaps the best feeling was that he knew he had been where no human had gone before.

3 Answer the questions

1 Where was the volcano?

....

2 How hot was it inside?

....

3 How long could you stay in the volcano without protection?

....

4 Where was Mackley born?

....

5 How long could he stay inside the volcano?

....

6 How far did he go into the volcano?

....

Vocabulary and Communication

Travel

 Complete the story with the verbs in the box.

leave   set off   get to   get off   take   get on

I bought myself a new bike so I could ride to work on it. It's not easy, but I enjoy doing it.

I always [1] .... at about 6.30. In the winter, it's really hard because it's so dark, but I have a lot of lights on my bike. It's important to go early because I need to catch a train. My office is 30 km from my home and I can't cycle that much every day! I [2] .... the train station at about 6.45, just in time for the 6.50 train. That train is great because there aren't many people on it. If I catch a later train, everyone gets angry at me for taking my bike on the train.

I [3] .... the train with my bike and sit down. These morning journeys [4] .... about 40 minutes and sometimes I can sleep. When it arrives, I [5] .... the train and [6] .... the station. Then, I cycle another 10 minutes to the office.

Talking about your journey to school

  Circle the words to complete the dialogue below. Then listen and check.

Harry How do you get to school every day?

Kate My dad takes me [1]*to / by* car to the bus stop then I get [2]*to / on* any bus – they all go [3] *past / on* my school from there.

Harry So what time do you set off in the morning?

Kate I get [4]*up / on* at about seven, and we get [5]*out of / into* the car at about quarter to eight.

Harry Does the bus stop right outside school?

Kate No. When I get [6]*out / off* the bus, I have to walk [7]*for / on* about three minutes.

Harry What time do you arrive at school?

Kate [8] *In / At* about quarter to nine.

Sounds right Weak forms in questions

  Listen to these questions. Notice that we don't pronounce *do* or *does* clearly unless it is at the start of the question. Repeat the questions.

1 Do you go to school every day?
2 So what time do you set off in the morning?
3 Does the bus stop right outside your school?
4 What time do you arrive at school?

Grammar

Past continuous vs Past simple

1 Match the sentences to the pictures.

1 The teacher told me off after I laughed out loud.
2 The teacher was telling me off when I laughed out loud.
3 When I got home, my dad cooked dinner.
4 When I got home, my dad was cooking dinner.

2 Complete the sentences with the Past simple or Past continuous form of the verbs in brackets.

1 When I .... (meet) Sally, she .... (work) in a café.
2 I .... (walk) down the street when I .... (trip) over.
3 He .... (eat) some Chinese food when his tooth .... (fall) out.
4 We .... (drive) down the street when we .... (see) a strange man standing in the road.
5 When I .... (get) home, my parents .... (sleep).
6 The last time I .... (see) Laura, she .... (make) a TV documentary.
7 Tom .... (try) to send a text message when his battery .... (die).
8 Mark and Lucy .... (watch) TV when they .... (hear) a strange noise outside the window.

Past perfect

3 Circle the action that happened first in each sentence.

1 I couldn't sleep because I had drunk too much coffee.
2 I had already lived in three different countries by the time I was 21.
3 We got a very cheap hotel room because we'd booked it very early.
4 They had known each other for four years before they got married.
5 They had seen the film at the cinema but they watched it again on DVD because they loved it.
6 She'd travelled for two hours before she realised she was on the wrong train.
7 Before the argument, Dave and James had been very good friends.

Grammar

4 Complete the sentences with the verbs below.

> hadn't been   had stopped   hadn't eaten   wasn't   stopped   didn't eat

1 I was scared, because I .... on a plane before.
2 I .... anything at the airport – I wasn't hungry.
3 By the time we got home, the rain ....
4 Anne phoned me to say that she .... on the train – she was taking a bus instead.
5 I .... sushi before I went to Japan.
6 While we were driving home, we .... to buy some petrol.

Narrative tenses (revision)

5 Circle the verbs to complete the story.

I wish I had stayed at home!

The first time I took a plane, it was a disaster! I ¹*got / was getting* to the airport very early because I was nervous about being late or missing the flight. So I ²*waited / had waited* a long time for the check-in to open.

Then, a message popped up on the screen that the plane had been delayed by two hours. So, I waited for another two hours. Then, after another two hours, another message ³*came / was coming* up saying that the plane was now an extra two hours late! This continued and continued ... All the passengers went to the information desk to find out what was happening, but nobody ⁴*was knowing / knew* anything. In the end, the plane was 24 hours late! Why the airline ⁵*doesn't tell / hadn't told* us at the beginning, I just don't know.

Anyway, while I was ⁶*waiting / had waited*, I spent a lot of money on food and drink and ⁷*read / was reading* three magazines.

In the end, the plane took off. I ⁸*wasn't sleeping / didn't sleep* at all while we were flying. I was too anxious.

The plane ⁹*was landing / landed* three times in three different countries. Because it ¹⁰*was arriving / arrived* late, I had to wait extra time for my connecting flights. So, by the time I arrived at my final destination, I ¹¹*didn't sleep / hadn't slept* for about three days. I ¹²*was only eating / had only eaten* in planes or airports and I wished I had never left home!

Skills

Reading

1 Read the article quickly and tick (✓) the best summary below.

1 There are lots of dangerous places on Earth. ☐
2 There are still lots of places to explore on Earth. ☐
3 There are many strange animals in the world. ☐

Maybe you think that humans have been to every corner of the world, that there is nowhere left to explore. No more new countries or secret places. If we want to see new things, we need to go into outer space and visit alien planets like Mars.

However, there are, in fact, many places here on Earth which we know very little about.

Papua New Guinea

This is a hot, tropical country of 7 million people in the South Pacific ocean. It is also one of the least explored countries in the world. It has high mountains, volcanoes and deep jungles. There are some places which haven't been touched by people – deep valleys which you can only visit by helicopter. Scientists are still discovering new species there – beautiful fish, frogs, large reptiles, and new animals like the tree kangaroo. Some scientists believe that up to 8% of all the world's species live in Papua New Guinea. And who knows how many more animals might be living in the deep jungles? Unfortunately, like the Amazon rainforest, trees are being cut down here, destroying the natural environment.

Antarctica

This is, of course, the coldest place on Earth. There are no cities here. The only animals which can live here need to be near the sea. And this is the only continent in the world which has no trees. You might think that this huge empty land has nothing but snow and ice. However, we now know that under the thick ice are hundreds of underground lakes. The largest is Lake Vostok, which is about 500 metres below the ice. Scientists drilled down to this lake and found that the water was 25 million years old. No one knows what is under Antarctica – perhaps there are unusual forms of life which we have never seen before!

The Mariana Trench

Most of the Earth is covered by water. And the most unexplored parts of our planet are the oceans. We know that the deepest part of the sea is the Mariana Trench. This is an incredible 11 kilometres deep and is located north of Papua New Guinea. It is difficult for humans to go down this deep, because it is very dangerous. Only a few people have tried. We don't really know what lives at the bottom of the oceans. Not only is it difficult to travel there but it is also completely dark. We do know that there are strange sharks, giant crabs, and very unusual creatures such as the angler fish. This unusual (and scary!) fish has a light growing out of its head which it uses to catch its food. There are probably many more species down there, waiting to be discovered.

2 Read the sentences and circle T (True) or F (False).

1 There are places in Papua New Guinea where people have never been. **T / F**
2 Most of the world's species live in Papua New Guinea. **T / F**
3 The coldest city in the world is in Antarctica. **T / F**
4 Scientists have found new life living under the ice in Antarctica. **T / F**
5 Not many people have been to the bottom of the oceans. **T / F**

Skills

Listening

09 CD1 **3** Listen and tick (✓) the photo the speaker is talking about.

10 CD1 **4** Listen again and match the numbers to the correct information.

1	5,000	a	the number of people living on this continent
2	1911	b	the number of months they travelled
3	two	c	the year a base was built here
4	1957	d	the first time anyone reached this place
5	less than 50	e	the temperature in the winter
6	-90	f	the number of people in this base in the winter

Writing

5 Read the travel advert. Would you like to go on this unusual holiday?

Antarctica

Travel to the end of the world!

Colder and windier than any other place on Earth – Antarctica feels like another world. Huge mountains of ice, penguins, incredible experiences. This will be the adventure of a lifetime!

We take small groups on a sea journey from Chile to the tip of Antarctica. You will spend 15 days on board our boat with all food included. Scientific experts will explain the unique Antarctic landscape as you travel the 800 km journey, and will even help you spot whales.

6 Imagine that your friend went on this holiday. Make a list of questions you would like to ask.

Did you like being on a boat for two weeks?
What animals did you see?

7 Now write an email to your friend in 100 words and ask your questions.

Deciding how to read

When we read something, we don't have to read every word to understand the meaning. Sometimes, we only need to look quickly at a text or find the parts that we need.

> ### Tips
>
> - To get a general idea of what you are reading about, try **skimming** it (reading it quickly). Use headlines, pictures or photos to help you.
> - To look for information, try **scanning** (looking through the text to find where the information is).
> - If you see a word you don't understand, ask 'Do I need to understand this word? Is it important?' If the answer is 'no', then continue reading!

 Skim the article at the bottom of the page quickly (in one minute) to find out what it is about. Do not read it in detail! Circle T (True) or F (False) for the sentences below.

The article ....

1 is about famous travellers.	**T / F**
2 is about an island.	**T / F**
3 is about the animals that live there.	**T / F**
4 says where the island is, and what it is like there.	**T / F**

2a **Now scan the article for information. Circle all the numbers in the article, then match the numbers to the information they describe. Spend about two minutes on this.**

a when TV first arrived here

b the distance from another country

c the number of people who live here

d the height of the volcano

e how often it rains

f how long people have lived here

g the length of the island

h when the volcano was last active

2b **Now look at the underlined words in the article. Did you need to understand these words to complete exercises 1 and 2?**

Tristan Da Cunha
– the world's most remote island

<u>Secluded and beguiling</u>, there are few places more lonely than the island of Tristan Da Cunha. Situated in the Atlantic Ocean, far from any other country – further than any other place in the world. It is 2,816 kilometres from the nearest land (South Africa), and it doesn't have an airport. The only way to get here is by boat.

Amazingly, people have lived here for more than 200 years. The first <u>permanent settlers</u> arrived in the 19th century. Now, the population is small – about 300 people. Life is simple here. There was no TV until 2001, and the internet arrived a few years later.

If you want to travel around Tristan Da Cunha, it won't take long! It's only 12 kilometres from north to south! The best way to get around is by walking. But the most interesting feature of the island is the volcano in the middle. It is 2,062 metres high, and when it last erupted in 1961, it was necessary for the island to <u>be evacuated.</u>

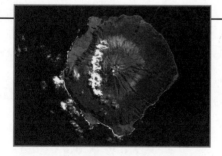

The weather here is usually cool, and wet – around 252 days every year are rainy. But if you have the time (and money), Tristan Da Cunha is an <u>intriguing destination</u> – far from the rest of the world, it is a <u>unique glimpse</u> into another way of life.

Exam skills 1

Speaking

 1 **Read this email from a friend, then look at the six pictures. Tick (✓) the things your friend should take.**

Hi!
I'm going hiking in the mountains next weekend. I've never been before! I know that you were in the mountains last year. What do you think I should take with me? It will be very high up and quite cold – it might even snow ...
Thanks,
Ben

2 **Now make a list of other things your friend should take. Talk about the things with a partner. Try to explain why these things are important.**

Tip Give examples from your own experience, if possible.

He should take a torch with batteries. When I went hiking, it got dark very quickly and I needed some light to see where I was going.

Writing

 3 **Your teacher has asked you to write a story. Follow the instructions below.**

- The title for your story is: *A travel adventure*. Two people are travelling somewhere.
- First, think about the characters and places you want in your story. Choose from the ideas below or use your own.

a handsome young man	a woman with a secret	a friendly old man	a detective
a foreign spy	a helicopter pilot	a photographer	a train
an animal expert	a jungle	the bottom of the sea	
a volcano	a plane at 30,000 feet	the South Pole	

- Now make notes on these questions.

Where are the two characters travelling, and why?	
What are the characters doing when they meet?	
What had they done before they met?	
What problem do they have?	
How do they solve the problem in the end?	

- Write your story in about 200 words. Remember to use narrative tenses. Show your story to your teacher.

Dialogue work

1 Complete the dialogue with the phrases below. Then listen and check.

> if you know what I mean   you shouldn't   Have you been   you ought to   I prefer   I think

Katie I love what you're wearing, Nicola!
¹ .... on a shopping spree? Everything's new!

Nicola Well, yes, everything's new to me but none of these clothes are actually new,
² ....

Katie Really? You mean they're second-hand clothes? I'd never buy anything someone else has worn.

Nicola Well, ³ .... – buying used things is a great way to recycle, and to save money. That's why I think online auction sites are such an amazing invention. I mean, it's such a waste, buying new things all the time when you could reuse something else.

Katie ⁴ .... paying for things in cash. At least people can't get all your bank details if you just hand over lots of money.

Nicola Oh, ⁵ .... it's perfectly safe to give your debit card details to websites that have good security. But I agree, ⁶ .... give your bank details to everyone. Especially not online. It can be very dangerous.

2 Write *Katie* or *Nicola*.

Who ...

1 often buys recycled clothes? ....
2 doesn't trust debit cards? ....
3 buys things online? ....
4 prefers to pay in cash? ....

3 Circle the correct words.

1 You *should / shouldn't* tell your password to anyone.
2 My shoes are really old – I *should / shouldn't* buy some new ones.
3 I've got a headache – I *ought to / shouldn't* use the computer so much.
4 I want to buy a nice pair of jeans – but first, I *should / shouldn't* save up some money.
5 You *ought to / shouldn't* try this new website – it's much cheaper than the shops.
6 If you think someone has your bank details, you *ought to / shouldn't* tell the bank immediately.

Vocabulary and Communication

Money and shopping

1 Complete the sentences with the correct word, then match them to the pictures below.

1 I bought this coat s_ _ _ _ _-_ _ _ _. It was much cheaper than a new one!
2 I bought this T-shirt for £50 in a shop, but then saw it on the internet for only £25!
  What a w_ _ _ _ of money!
3 Look at her with all those bags – she's been on a shopping s_ _ _ _!
4 Sorry, we don't accept cards – just c_ _ _ _.
5 I shop o_ _ _ _ _ for a lot of things – tickets, books, etc. It's easier than going to the shops!
6 I don't want to buy anything. I just want to go w_ _ _ _ _ s_ _ _ _ _ _ _

Talking about shopping

2 Complete these dialogues with the words below. Then listen and check.

only	on	found	window	by	take

1 **Customer** These fit me very well. I'll [1] .... them. Can I pay [2] .... debit card?
  Assistant Sorry, it's cash [3] .... No cheques or cards.

2 **Sam** What an amazing jacket!
  Jo I know. It's a genuine 1950s one. I [4] .... it in a second-hand shop.

3 **Claudia** I hope you're not planning to go [5] .... a shopping spree. I haven't got any money at all.
  Amy Neither have I, but we can always [6] .... shop.

Grammar

should(n't) / ought(n't)

1 Complete the dialogues with the phrases below.

get a new one   apologise   get your hair cut   keep them in a safe place

❶ I keep losing my keys.

You should ....

❷ I feel bad about being so rude to John.

You should ....

❸ I can't read this book.

You should ....

❹ My computer keeps crashing!

You should ....

2 Complete the sentences with *should, shouldn't* or *ought*.

1 **A** I feel so tired these days.
  B You .... to go to bed earlier.
2 **A** I think I'm going to be ill.
  B OK, well, you .... go out tonight.
3 **A** I ordered a new laptop online, and it hasn't arrived.
  B You .... email or phone the company, and find out what happened.
4 **A** It's my mother's birthday tomorrow.
  B You .... buy her something nice.
5 **A** I don't have any winter clothes.
  B You .... to buy yourself a good coat.

3 Rewrite the second sentence so that it has the same meaning as the first. Use the words in brackets.

1 The best thing to do is phone the company and find out what happened. (ought)
  You ....
2 John is the person to speak to if your computer is broken. (should)
  You ....
3 Listening to songs in English can help you improve your speaking skills. (ought)
  You ....
4 It isn't a good idea to spend too long in front of a computer. (shouldn't)
  You ....
5 It's not nice to forget someone's birthday. (shouldn't)
  You ....
6 Take an umbrella – it's raining. (should)
  You ....

Grammar

Gerunds

4 Complete the sentences with the verbs below.

> buying   spending   giving   paying   shopping   saving

1 Window .... is a really cheap way to spend time because you don't buy anything!
2 .... money is very important if you want to buy something expensive.
3 He loves .... money on the latest fashions.
4 I prefer .... for things in cash, not with a credit card.
5 .... your bank details to someone is a big mistake!
6 .... second-hand clothes is a good way to save money.

5 Complete the sentences with the gerund form of the verb in brackets.

1 I love .... I spend every weekend baking something. (cook)
2 I have to do my homework tonight. .... Maths is the worst! (study)
3 Jon loves .... He wants to go to drama school one day. (act)
4 It is hard for foreign tourists to get used to .... on the left in Britain. (drive)
5 After .... here, I made new friends very quickly. (come)
6 .... ill is the worst thing in the world! (be)

6 Read Rachel's answers to the questionnaire below then complete the text.

Do you play a musical instrument?	Yes – guitar. I practise every day.
Do you listen to music?	Yes, all the time. I love it.
Do you exercise?	No, never. I don't like it.
Do you help your parents at home?	Yes, every weekend I tidy my room.
Do you often go shopping for clothes?	Yes, I love clothes!

Rachel's regular activities include [1] .... the guitar, [2] .... to music, [3] .... her room and [4] .... for clothes. She doesn't like [5] ....

Skills

Reading

1 **Read the article about shopping. Complete the gaps with the correct headings.**

a Decide how much you want to spend.

b Check it carefully before you buy.

c Take a friend with you.

d Decide exactly what you need.

e Trust your feelings.

f Ask for help.

How to go shopping!

Have you ever bought something, then when you took it home, realised you had made a mistake?
Have you ever bought the wrong thing by accident?
Have you ever wasted an afternoon checking all the shops before finding what you need?
Do you have problems deciding what to buy?
Read our useful tips, and save yourself lots of time and money!

1 ....

It's very easy to go shopping and buy extra things you don't really need. So, before you go, you ought to know exactly how much money you have, and how much you can afford. If you don't do this, you might spend more money than you want.

2 ....

This relates to the point above. Before you go out, think about what you want to buy. Check prices and designs online. Write down the names and the prices of the things you want. If you don't do this, then you might waste a lot of time looking for things.

3 ....

This is very important. If you're buying clothes, then you should try them on before you buy them! If you're buying some electronic equipment, look at it very closely. Are there any scratches, or does it look in bad condition? Then don't buy it!

4 ....

Shop assistants are there for a reason. They are there for the customers – you! If you need to know something, or you can't find what you want, then you ought to speak to a member of staff. That's their job!

5 ....

If you need to buy a new dress, or an expensive new piece of equipment, you should bring someone with you. Firstly, they can help you make a good decision and tell you what looks good and what doesn't. Secondly, it's a lot more fun!

6 ....

Finally, if you have a bad feeling about something, or you're just not 100% sure, then don't buy it! You should listen to your heart. Only you can decide if you want to spend your money or not!

2 **Read the article again. Complete the sentences below with *should* or *shouldn't*.**

1 You .... think about how much money you have before you go shopping.

2 You .... check things on the internet before you go shopping.

3 You .... buy things without trying them on first.

4 You .... speak to people in shops.

5 You .... go to the shops alone.

6 You .... buy something if you have doubts about it.

Skills

Listening

3 Listen to someone reading an article about shopping. Tick (✓) the best title below.

1 Should we buy things we don't really need? ☐
2 Does shopping make you happier? ☐
3 The problem with shopping sprees. ☐

4 Match the sentence halves. Then listen again and check.

1 Some people try to make themselves feel happier
2 Most adults have gone shopping
3 Shop owners know that people
4 Perhaps people do this
5 But money can't
6 The positive effects of shopping

a when they feel unhappy.
b to feel more in control of their lives.
c buy happiness.
d by shopping.
e don't last very long.
f like to buy more things when they are sad.

5 Writing

Think of something you bought recently. Answer the questions below.

1 What did you buy?
2 When and where did you buy it?
3 Why did you choose it?
4 How did it make you feel when you bought it?
5 Would you like to buy something similar again?
6 Would you recommend this item to other people?

6 Use your answers to write about 150 words about the thing you bought.

Text work

1 Read the interviews and write the jobs next to the correct person below.

1 testing DVDs
2 testing computer games
3 testing recipes
4 playing historical characters
5 selling ice cream to tourists

2 Read the interviews again and circle the correct words.

My worst ever job!

We asked five people to tell us about a job they used to do, and why it was so bad ...

A Maria: ....

It was just ¹*when / before* the Christmas season. Our job was to play them until they broke. It sounds more fun than it actually was. Just you try to listen to a character saying the same things over and over for three weeks. It drives you insane!

B Paul: ....

²*When / As soon as* I was at drama school, I had a holiday job at a famous attraction in England. I had to dress up as King Henry VIII all through the hot summer. ³*Before / As soon as* the tourists went home, I used to strip off my costume and dive into the fountains.

C Jenny: ....

I got it ⁴*before / when* someone who was working for a big food company saw me and my friend in the supermarket, trying the free samples. The next thing was, I was being paid to do it. Basically, the only skill you needed was a big appetite. It was fine for a while but then I started feeling ill because I was eating too much.

D: David: ....

At first, because I'm completely mad about films, I thought it was the best job ever. But ⁵*before / after* working several night shifts, I was so tired in the mornings, I couldn't remember what I'd seen.

E: Olivia: ....

It was at a big seaside resort. The good thing was meeting lots of people. The bad thing was that the wind would sometimes blow it into your face, hair and eyes. It was so sticky. I always had to have a long shower ⁶*as soon as / before* I got home.

Vocabulary and Communication

Personality adjectives

1 Write the personality adjectives under the correct picture.

| polite | hard-working | easy-going | creative | friendly | helpful |

....

....

Talking about personality and jobs

2 Rewrite the sentences changing the words in bold.

1 A good waiter has to be **rude** and **unfriendly**. ....

....

2 You need to be **lazy** if you want to be a farmer. ....

....

3 A sports coach has to be **impatient**. ....

....

4 Teachers need to be **unhelpful** with their students. ....

....

5 Police officers should be **dishonest** and **irresponsible** people. ....

....

Sounds right Word stress

3 Circle the syllables that are stressed in the words in exercise 1. Then listen and check.

Grammar

Talking about the future

1 Decide if these sentences are talking about arrangements (A) or intentions (I). Circle A or I below.

1 My brother is a student now, but when he finishes university,
   he is going to be an engineer.   **A / I**
2 I'm visiting the dentist tomorrow.   **A / I**
3 I don't know any Japanese, but I'm going to study it.   **A / I**
4 I'm going to try much harder at school from now on.   **A / I**
5 I'm meeting my friends tonight.   **A / I**
6 She's having her hair cut this afternoon.   **A / I**

2 Look at Suzy's diary and complete the sentences with the Present continuous form of the verbs.

Tomorrow
06:00 Go to the gym.
09:00 Take exam. Maths!
12:00 Lunch.
13:00 Do English exam …
15:00 Go home – relax!
16:00 Meet Anna and Charlie.
17:00 Party!

Suzy has a busy day tomorrow – but she has planned everything. She ¹.................... (go) to the gym at 6 am so she is early for school. She ².................... (revise) at school because she ³.................... (take) a Maths exam at 9 am. After lunch, she ⁴.................... (do) an English exam. Then, she ⁵.................... (meet) Anna and Charlie in the afternoon and they ⁶.................... (go) to a party.

3 Complete these intentions with *going to* and a verb from below.

tell	join	buy	get	not take	not go

1 I need to lose weight. I .... a gym.
2 They don't have a lot of money, so they .... on holiday this year.
3 Jack's computer is broken, so he .... a new one.
4 We've made a decision. Next year, we .... married!
5 I .... the bus to school any more – I have a new bike.
6 She's decided to leave her job. She .... her boss tomorrow.

Grammar

Future time clauses

4 **Circle the correct words.**

1 *As soon as / Before* you travel to the US, you need to get a visa.

2 I always have a snack *after / before* getting home from school.

3 What are you doing *before / when* school finishes today?

4 We *will speak / speak* to him before he leaves.

5 I *will learn / learn* how to drive after I finish my exams.

5 **Circle the correct verbs.**

1 When I get home tonight, I *phone / will phone* you.

2 As soon as I *find out / will find out* what happened, I'll tell you.

3 Before I *go / will go* to school, I always have a big breakfast.

4 I usually do my homework after I *finish / will finish* my dinner.

6 **Complete the second sentence so that it has a similar meaning to the first. Use the words below.**

| after | as soon as | before | when |

1 The minute I get home, I'll phone you.

I'll phone you .... I get home.

2 I'll definitely visit the Taj Mahal the next

time I go to India. .... I go

to India, I'll definitely visit the Taj Mahal.

3 Are you going to revise earlier for your exams?

Are you going to revise .... your exams?

4 What are we going to do when the exams are finished?

What are we going to do .... the exams?

7 **Write four sentences using the words from exercise 6.**

1 ....

2 ....

3 ....

4 ....

Skills

Reading

1 Read the article quickly. Circle True (T) or False (F) for the sentences below.

The future of work

We asked two business experts to tell us how things will change.

Theo Manatos

Remember that things have changed a lot in recent years. Not so long ago, we didn't have social networks – we didn't even have the internet or emails. So just imagine how things will change in the next 20 years. We're all going to need to be computer experts in the future. If you don't know how to use a computer, well, you're going to be in trouble. We will spend more time in front of our laptops or tablets, and work isn't going to be a place you go. Work is going to be something you do – at home, in cafés, it doesn't matter – and at any time. Our colleagues will be all over the world – we won't even meet most of them. Our idea of working regular times – Monday to Friday, from 9 to 5 – will change. This means that we will spend more time with our families, and that will mean big changes for everyone.

Angela Sharpe

I agree with Theo. At the moment, there are far more men than women in senior positions. There are more male managers, company owners and even presidents and prime ministers. In my opinion, this will change – slowly, but it will change. In about 20 years' time, I believe that we will see a more equal balance of men and women in top jobs. And this means that men are going to be spending a lot more time at home looking after the children. It will become more and more normal for a man to spend time taking care of his family, spending less time at work. And this means that women will be applying for jobs that, traditionally, only men have applied for.

1 The article is about how working habits will change. **T / F**
2 It is about working in different countries. **T / F**
3 It mentions how people worked 100 years ago. **T / F**
4 It mentions how men and women's lives will change. **T / F**

2 Read the article again and answer the questions.

1 Theo thinks that we need to learn IT skills because
   A most of our work will be based around computers.
   B computer programmers will make the most money.
   C more women will be computer experts.

2 According to Theo, our lives will change because
   A we won't make so much money.
   B we will be more lonely.
   C we won't have regular working hours or workplaces.

3 Angela believes that in the future,
  A women will have better opportunities at work.
  B women will spend more time with men.
  C only women will be presidents and prime ministers.

4 She thinks that women will
  A apply for more jobs previously done by men.
  B will share more jobs with men at home.
  C will stay at home.

Listening

 3 Listen and match the jobs of the future to the pictures.

1 vertical farming
2 elderly care specialist
3 hologram management
4 time banking

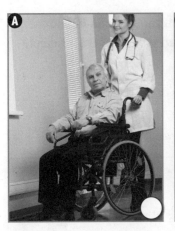

 4 Listen again and complete the summary with words from the presentation.

space   citizens   money   virtual

We will need vertical farming, because there will be less [1] .... and we might need to farm in high buildings.

The number of senior [2] .... will increase and we will need specialists to look after the elderly.

We will have more [3] .... friends who will speak to us and help us.

In the future, time will be more valuable than [4] ...., and we will need people to help us keep it safe.

Writing

5 Think about a job you might like in the future. Make notes on these questions.

1 What is the job? What will you have to do?
2 Where will you work (at home, in an office, outside, etc.)?
3 Who will your colleagues be?
4 How long would you like to do this job?

6 Write a paragraph about your dream job.

Learning to learn (Units 3 and 4)

Dealing with unknown words

When you read in English, you will often find words you don't know. If you check every word you don't understand in a dictionary, it will take a lot of time. Lots of very new words might not even appear in a dictionary!

Tips

1 Decide if the word is important. Do you really need to know what it means? If not, ignore it!
2 Is the word a verb, a noun or an adjective? Is it part of a phrase?
3 Try looking at the words in the sentence. Sometimes, the context (the other information around the word) can help you understand what it might mean.

 Read this article about future jobs quickly. There are some important words in the article which are unusual or perhaps difficult. Look at underlined words 1–6 and circle the type of word you think they are.

1 coffice: *verb / noun / adjective*
2 grim: *verb / noun / adjective*
3 breakneck: *verb / noun / adjective*

4 blanketed: *verb / noun / adjective*
5 soonologist: *verb / noun / adjective*
6 company: *verb / noun / adjective*

The ¹Coffice – Workplace of the Future

Where will we work in the future? Well, according to many experts, we won't be working in a boring, ²grim office building. Instead, we'll be able to take our laptops wherever we want!

Thanks to modern developments, our wifi is improving at ³breakneck speeds. For example, in Seoul (the capital of South Korea), the whole city is ⁴blanketed in free wifi spots – and internet speeds are so fast there, that you can download entire films in a few seconds. Wherever you are these days, you're never far away from a wifi hotspot, which means you can work anywhere, anytime.

According to one ⁵soonologist, Nicola Millard, the 'coffice' will be the workplace of the future. It has four very important things to keep workers happy: great coffee, cakes, good ⁶company, and of course, free wifi.

Now match words 1–6 with definitions a–f.

1 coffice   a   a person who studies technology to predict the near future
2 grim   b   a café where we can do our work
3 breakneck   c   being with other people
4 blanket   d   very fast
5 soonologist   e   ugly and unpleasant
6 company   f   to cover something completely

Exam skills 2

Speaking

1 Look at these jobs. In pairs, talk about which jobs you would prefer to do and why.

 pilot

 writer

 charity worker

 software designer

 singer

 journalist

Tip Remember to give reasons for your opinions, not only short answers.

> I wouldn't like to be a writer, because I prefer working with other people.

> I'd rather be a singer than a charity worker, because I want to be famous and have lots of money.

Reading

2 Read about six people who would like to change their job in the future. Decide which job from exercise 1 would be best for each person.

 1 Kaya has always had a great voice. He used to be in band when he was at school, and he plays a lot of musical instruments. He loves performing and would prefer a job where he can be artistic.

 2 Roberto is good with words. He always watches the news and keeps up to date with what's happening in the world. He wants a job where he can work with other people and use his writing skills.

 3 Rachel has always loved travelling. Her first travel experience was flying from London to Australia. Since then, she has loved flying. She is very good with people and can always stay calm in stressful situations.

 4 Akash would rather spend his time helping other people than making lots of money. He usually spends a few hours at the weekend doing voluntary work at his local hospital, and believes that everybody should give something back to society.

 5 Clara is a very artistic person and likes creating stories. She spends most of her free time reading and has a great idea for a new children's book. Her dream is to put all her ideas down on paper and find someone who would like to publish her stories.

 6 Chen doesn't like working with other people very much. She prefers spending her time with a computer to doing sports or going to parties. She's extremely good at Maths and problem-solving, and you can usually find her playing on her tablet or phone.

Dialogue work

1 Complete the dialogue with the words below.

so	character	such	exciting	novel	author	put

Karen I'm in ¹ .... a bad mood.

Greg What is it, what's the problem?

Karen This is ² .... annoying!

Greg What?

Karen This book I'm reading – this detective ³ .... – the last page is missing on this e-reader! Now I can't find out which ⁴ .... was the murderer! I've been reading this book for two days – I couldn't ⁵ .... it down – and now I can't finish it!

Greg Have you tried turning it off and on again?

Karen I've tried everything, but it's stuck on page 239. I want to know what happens on page 240!

Greg OK, but it's not such a big problem.

Karen Yes, it is! Now I won't be able to stop thinking about what happens at the end!

Greg Maybe the ⁶ .... really did stop on page 239. Maybe she wanted to make everyone guess what happens!

Karen That's such a stupid thing to say.

Greg OK. Stop being such a bookworm. Let's go to the cinema instead. It's the weekend!

Karen No, no. I want to find out ... Hang on ... wait ... OK! It works. Now I can see page 240. Wow! So the murderer was ... Wow – that's so ⁷ ....

Greg Who? Who? Tell me! Who was the murderer? Not the butler again?

Karen Sorry. I'm not telling you. You'll have to read it to find out.

2 Answer the questions.

1 Why was Karen in a bad mood?

....

2 What did Karen want to find out?

....

3 What did Greg say the author wanted to do?

....

4 What did Greg suggest they do?

....

5 Why didn't Karen tell Greg who the murderer was?

....

Vocabulary and Communication

Types of book

1 Read the clues and complete the puzzle about types of book. Then find the mystery word.

1 a novel which uses pictures, rather than words
2 a novel about people who solve crimes
3 this is not long – about 10,000 words in length (two words)
4 a book about someone's life
5 a piece of writing with short lines, and words which sound the same
6 a story about love

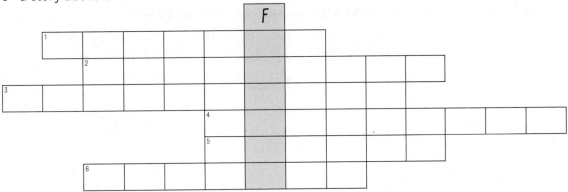

Talking about books

19

2 Complete the dialogue with the words below. You do not need to use all the words. Then listen and check.

crime	character	novels	all right	find out	put down	favourite

Nick Do you like graphic [1] .... ?

Eva What do you mean – *Coraline*, something like that?

Nick Yes. It's my [2] .... kind of book.

Eva Mmm, they're [3] .... but I'm not mad about them.

Nick So what do you like, then?

Eva I like books that are exciting, when you just can't wait to [4] .... what happens in the end.

Nick Do you like detective novels, and [5] .... , that sort of thing?

Eva Yes, I love that kind of book.

Sounds right Compound word stress

20

3 Circle the stress in the words below then listen and check.

1 short story
2 non-fiction
3 graphic novel
4 book cover
5 e-reader

Grammar

so / such

1 **Circle the correct word.**

1 I was *so / such* tired that I couldn't stay awake.
2 The film was *so / such* boring that I didn't stay until the end.
3 It was *so / such* a bad meal that I had to ask to speak to the manager.
4 I've got *so / such* a lot of homework, I won't be able to come out this weekend.
5 It was *so / such* a hot day yesterday, wasn't it?
6 He's got *so / such* much energy – he never sits still!

2 **Complete the sentences with *so*, *such* and the words below.**

a stormy	hungry	a sad	difficult	a good	fast

1 I ate all the food in two minutes because I was ....
2 She drove .... that she nearly had an accident.
3 He was .... author that everyone wanted to read his books.
4 It was .... night that I couldn't sleep.
5 The exam was .... that I couldn't answer the questions.
6 It was .... book – I couldn't stop crying.

3 **Write sentences about the pictures using *so* and *such*.**

1 It / cold / I / wear / all my winter clothes.

....

....

2 It / a great holiday / we / not want / to leave.

....

....

3 The food / good / I / eat / everything

....

....

Grammar

Phrasal verbs

4 Complete the phrasal verbs with a preposition from the box.

> up   off (x2)   out   back   down

1 Please can you turn your computer .... when you finish using it?
2 When I took .... running, I was surprised how difficult it was.
3 My plane took .... three hours late!
4 It was such an exciting book, I couldn't put it ....
5 Jon and Amee fell .... after they had an argument.
6 By the time we got .... , it was midnight.

5 Match the underlined phrasal verbs to the correct meanings.

1 Can you <u>turn up</u> the sound, please? I can't hear anything.
2 Michael always <u>turns up</u> late – he should buy himself a watch.
3 Prices are <u>going up</u> – I was shocked how expensive everything was in the shop.
4 He's <u>going up</u> the stairs – quick, catch him!
5 This book is quite boring for the first two chapters, but you'll soon <u>get into</u> it.
6 As soon as you <u>get into</u> the taxi, tell the driver where you want to go.

a enter   ☐
b increase   ☐ ☐
c arrive   ☐
d become used to   ☐
e move higher   ☐

6 Circle the correct word.

1 There was so much information in the book that I couldn't take it all *out / in*.
2 You can borrow my laptop, but please look *before / after* it.
3 I thought the book would be boring, but it turned *out / down* to be excellent.
4 It's a good idea to look *around / over* your work before giving it to your teacher.
5 If you want to get fit, you should take *out / up* running.
6 The police ran *before / after* the robber, but they didn't catch him.
7 I don't know who wrote this book, but I'll look *onto / into* it.
8 I need to go to the dentist and have a tooth taken *out / off*.

Skills

Reading

 1 **Read these online reviews of a book. Who liked the book?**

Reviews

Alan 2 September

I may be unusual, because I had never heard of this book or this writer before I picked it up. But I thought it was a very good book. I enjoyed all of it, and read it very quickly. I can't wait to read more of this writer's work.

Fergus 13 September

I think this is worth reading. The story is clever – it has lots of unusual characters, even if some of them are not really likeable. Sometimes the story gets a bit boring and nothing much happens, but overall, it's a nice book to take with you on holiday. I'd recommend it to anyone who likes old-fashioned detective stories.

Krystal 24 September

Oh dear! I wanted to like this book after all the good reviews I heard about it. I downloaded it for a good price, and started reading it straight away. The first few chapters were amazing. Such brilliant characters, and a fantastic opening. I really wanted to know what happened next. But, unfortunately, the story just got more and more boring. Nothing happened! Some people think that this might be realistic (because in real life, not much happens) but I wanted more excitement. I'm sorry to say that I gave up half-way through the book.

Nella 25 September

Clever, smart, funny … These are words I would never use to describe this book! I've never read anything so stupid in my life! A detective story should keep you guessing until the end. But I worked out who the murdered person was in Chapter 2! What a waste of time.

Gina 31 September

This is one of my favourite books. I've read it three times now, and I always find something new in it every time. It's WONDERFUL. And don't listen to all the other negative reviewers. They have no idea what they are talking about.

2 **Circle T (True) or F (False) for the sentences below.**

1	This is the first book Alan has read by this writer.	**T / F**
2	Fergus thinks everything about the book is good.	**T / F**
3	He doesn't think other people should read this book.	**T / F**
4	Krystal loves this book.	**T / F**
5	She didn't finish it.	**T / F**
6	Nella doesn't think the book is clever or funny.	**T / F**
7	She think it's a bad example of a crime story.	**T / F**
8	Gina likes the writer, but is quite negative about the book.	**T / F**

Skills

Listening

21 · 3 Listen to Omar and Ashley filling in a survey about reading. Complete the survey below with one word in each gap.

> **Thank you for agreeing to do our survey. Please look at the statements below. Do you *strongly agree, agree, disagree* or *strongly disagree* with each one?**
>
> 1 Reading is more for .... than ....
> 2 Reading is ....
> 3 Reading is ....
> 4 I can't find books that .... me.
> 5 I prefer to .... my own books.

22 · 4 Listen again. For each question in exercise 3, decide if Omar and Ashley strongly agree (SA), agree (A), disagree (D) or strongly disagree (SD).

1 Omar **SA A D SD**, Ashley **SA A D SD**
2 Omar **SA A D SD**, Ashley **SA A D SD**
3 Omar **SA A D SD**, Ashley **SA A D SD**
4 Omar **SA A D SD**, Ashley **SA A D SD**
5 Omar **SA A D SD**, Ashley **SA A D SD**

Writing

5 Answer the questions in exercise 3 yourself. Give reasons for your opinions in the table below.

	Do you agree?	Reasons
Question 1		
Question 2		
Question 3		
Question 4		
Question 5		

6 Write a paragraph about reading. Use your notes from exercise 5.

UNIT 6 The big occasion

Text work

1 **Read the article about the World Cup quickly. Tick the things that are mentioned below.**

The FIFA football World Cup is without doubt one of the biggest sporting events in the world. Every four years, 32 countries play each other to become the world football champion. Here are some interesting facts about this event, which you might not have known.

The first World Cup took place a very long time ago – in 1930. The South American country of Uruguay was the host, and only 13 teams took part. Most of these countries were from North or South America. Only four teams from Europe played: France, Belgium, Romania and Yugoslavia. There were no teams from Africa, Asia or Australia. This was because (in those days), travelling all the way to Uruguay was a very long and expensive journey!

Since then, there have been 19 World Cup tournaments. In this time, 77 different countries have taken part. But despite this, only eight countries have won the Cup: Brazil, Italy, Germany, Argentina, Uruguay, England, France and Spain. Brazil is the most successful footballing country – it has won the World Cup five times, and is the only team which has played in every tournament since 1930. The most successful footballer with the most goals is Brazil's Ronaldo.

The World Cup was first shown on television in 1954. Since then, it has become the most watched sporting occasion in the world. Nearly a billion people watched the last final match live – that's one in eight people across the world.

1 When the first World Cup was held. ☐
2 Who played in the first World Cup. ☐
3 The difference between men's football and women's football. ☐
4 The team which has won the most. ☐
5 Countries which have never played in the World Cup. ☐
6 How many people view the World Cup on television. ☐

2 **Complete the summary using information from the article.**

THE WORLD CUP
- a)..... countries compete every b)............................. years.

The first World Cup
- Took place in c)............................. in 1930.
- d) .... teams played.
- No teams from e) .... , Asia or Australia

1930 – present day
- 19 World Cup tournaments, and f) .... countries have played
- There have been g) .... winning countries.
- h) .... has won the most.

The World Cup on TV
- Broadcasts started in i)............................. .
- About j) .... watch the finals.

Vocabulary and Communication

Special events

1 Complete the words to make phrases about special events.

1 A fashion show is where models
2 A music festival is where you can see
3 A football match is where
4 Booksellers and writers show their
5 You can see running, jumping, etc.
6 The Oscars is a famous awards ceremony
7 A school fete is where
8 The Tour de France is

a latest works at a book fair.
b at an athletics competition.
c wear new styles of clothes.
d for people who make films.
e lots of bands playing.
f a famous cycling tournament.
g two teams play against each other.
h you can play games, buy things and meet your teachers!

2 Match the sentences in exercise 1 to the pictures below.

Talking about events

3 Listen to the dialogue. Circle the events that are mentioned in exercise 2 then complete the sentences.

1 .... to a rock festival?
2 What were they ....?
3 They're my .... band.
4 Yeah, I .... them, too.
5 I think modelling .... hard work, though.

Sounds right Word stress

4 Listen and circle the stress in the words below.

1 fashion
2 music
3 ceremony
4 competition

5 athletics
6 information
7 conversation
8 tournament

Grammar

The passive

1 Underline the passive in each sentence.

1 The Oscars <u>are held</u> every year in Hollywood.
2 I'm not allowed to go out before I've finished my homework.
3 Her new book was bought by millions of people around the world.
4 I think new designer fashion is only bought by rich people.
5 The robber was arrested last night by five police officers.
6 I wasn't invited to the party – were you?
7 The students were asked to sit down and open their books.
8 The festival was advertised everywhere in the city.

2 Match the sentences to the correct pictures. Then write P (Passive) or A (Active) next to each one.

1 An old woman was given £2,000,000 last week.
2 A robber was caught last night by two police officers.
3 A man bit a crocodile in the zoo yesterday.
4 An old woman gave £2,000,000 to charity last week.
5 A man was bitten by a crocodile in the zoo yesterday.
6 A robber caught two police officers last night.

3 Circle the correct verbs.

A history of tennis

Originally, tennis balls ¹ *made / were made* in Scotland from sheep stomachs. These early tennis balls ² *were stuffed / were stuff* with wool. In the 18th century, strips of wool ³ *was wrapped / were wrapped* tightly around a little ball. Then, string ⁴ *was tied / is tied* around the ball and the whole ball ⁵ *was covered / was cover* with a white cloth. Modern tennis balls ⁶ *are make / are made* from rubber. They ⁷ *are then covered / were then covered* with a soft material called felt.

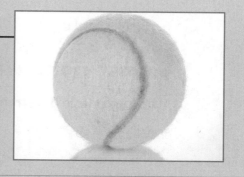

Grammar

make / let / be allowed to

4 Use the prompts below with the correct form of the verbs to write sentences and questions.

1 your parents / let / you / play computer games / ?

....

2 what time / your parents / usually / make / you / come home / ?

....

3 you / allow / go out / late at night / ?

....

4 we / not allow / wear / jewellery at school /.

....

5 coffee / make / me / feel ill /.

....

6 our teacher / make / us / work / so hard yesterday / !

....

7 my mum / not allow / me / miss / school unless I'm ill /.

....

8 John / always / let / me / borrow / his computer /.

....

5 Read the information and decide if the sentences are T (True) or F (False).

HOTEL PARADISE

Dear Guests!

We would like to welcome you to our hotel. Here is some information which will help you to have a nice stay.

- Please respect other guests and be quiet after 10 pm.
- Please telephone #8339 before 6 pm if you want to order some food in your room.
- Please give your room key to reception when you go out.
- The wi-fi password is PASSWORD12456%67.
- Your room will be cleaned once every two days.
- You can pay by cash or credit card.
- You must check out before 11 am.

1 You aren't allowed to make a noise late at night.	**T / F**
2 The hotel doesn't let you eat in the rooms.	**T / F**
3 You are allowed to take your room key with you when you go out.	**T / F**
4 You are allowed to use the internet.	**T / F**
5 The hotel makes you clean your own room every day.	**T / F**
6 The hotel only allows you to pay by credit card.	**T / F**
7 The hotel doesn't let you stay after 11 am when you leave.	**T / F**

Skills

Reading

 Read about three different festivals. Match the festivals to the correct photos.

❶ New Year Water Festival

The Songran festival takes place in Thailand at the start of each year. In this country, the year begins in April. The festival takes place during the hottest time of the year, so people walk around the streets throwing large amounts of water at each other. Water is thought to have a cleansing effect, and brings good luck. Sometimes, you can even see elephants [1] spraying water over crowds of people, or large trucks with water cannons!

❷ The World Gurning Championship

This is a uniquely English tradition, and not a very pretty one. The Egremont Crab Fair, in the north of England, has taken place since 1267. The fair is named after a fruit called the crab apple, which is very bitter, and makes your face change shape when you eat it. Contestants battle each other to see who can [2] contort their face the most. This bizarre sport is very often won by people who have no teeth as some of them can cover their noses with their mouths!

❸ The Living Chess Game

The small village of Marostica, near Venice in Italy, has a large chess board, framed by a beautiful old castle. Since the 15th century, a real-life chess game (with people dressed as the pieces, and real horses) has taken place every two years, on the second weekend in September. All the town's people come out and take part. According to one story, the game started in 1454, when two different men wanted to marry the daughter of Lord Taddeo Parisio. Instead of asking them to fight a [3] duel with each other to the death, the lord decided to hold a chess game, to find out who would be his new son-in-law.

2 Reread the articles and circle the correct meanings of the <u>underlined</u> words in the texts. Then check your answers in a dictionary.

1 spraying
  A spreading water over a large area
  B taking water from somewhere
  C giving water for someone else to drink

2 contort
  A hurting something
  B making something look beautiful
  C making something change shape in a strange way

3 duel
  A a fight between two people, using guns or swords
  B a friendly game
  C a serious discussion

Skills

Listening

3 Listen to a report about a festival and tick (✓) the correct photo.

26 **4** Listen again and complete column A in the table.

	A	B
What is the name of the festival?	1	
Which country does it take place in?	2	
How many people are in each team?	3	
What happens?	4	
How old is the festival?	5	
When does it take place?	6	
Why is the festival interesting?	7	

Writing

5 Think of a festival or special occasion that you have experienced or have heard about. Make notes in column B of the table above.

6 Write a paragraph about the festival or special occasion. Explain why you like it or you think it is interesting.

Note making

Note making is useful when you need to write down complicated information in a short way which is quick and easy to remember.

Making notes before we speak or write can help us plan our ideas better.

Tips

- When we make notes, we don't need to write full sentences.
- We can use bullet points or we can use abbreviations (like in a text message).
- No one will read the notes – only you! So it is OK to write in a style which only you understand!

  Listen to a talk about birthdays and complete the notes with the words and numbers below.

> China   Name Day   seaweed soup   5   7   3   Korea   New Year's Day

BIRTHDAYS AROUND THE WORLD
Food

- many countries, cake, sweets, chocs

- a).............................: noodles – long life

- Korea: b)................................ – v. healthy

Special numbers

- Japan: boys – c)................ , d)................ ; girls – e)................ ; 77 is lucky no.

- f)................ : 100 days after a child is born.

Other facts

- Vietnam: celebrate bday on g)................................

- Poland & Italy, etc: h)................................ important

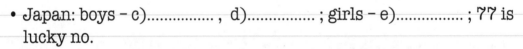

---

2 **Match the abbreviations from the notes to the correct meaning.**

1 chocs	a number
2 v.	b birthday
3 no.	c chocolates
4 bday	d and so on
5 &	e and
6 etc.	f very

 Now use the notes from exercise 1 to write a paragraph about birthdays around the world.

Exam skills 3

Speaking

1 Look at this photo of a special occasion. Make notes and describe the things you see.

The occasion	
The people	
What the people are doing	
How the people are feeling	
Other things you can see	

2 Tick the phrases you would use to describe the photo. What other phrases could you use?

- This picture shows … ☐
- He's wearing … ☐
- On the left, there's a … ☐

- In the middle, I can see … ☐
- He's probably feeling … ☐
- They seem to be … ☐

3 Practise describing the photo in exactly one minute.

Writing

4 Read part of an email you received from a friend.

Hi there, I'm doing a project on special occasions. Do you remember a special occasion from when you were a child – like a birthday or another kind of celebration? What was it like? What happened, and who was there? Did you enjoy it?

5 Write back to your friend. Describe a special occasion. Follow the instructions below.

- Use friendly, informal language.
- Write a paragraph of about 100 words.
- When you finish, check your work for mistakes.

Dialogue work

28 1 Circle the correct words in the dialogue. Then listen and check.

Holly It's Steve's birthday tomorrow, [1]*isn't it / doesn't it*?

Joanne Oh – you're right. It is. [2]*Will / Won't* there be a party?

Holly Yes, there will. Everyone's invited. You'll come, [3]*won't you / aren't you*?

Joanne Sure. Let's get him a present.

Holly Well, I was thinking about taking him some food.

Joanne Food? You mean buy him some chocolates, or something?

Holly No, I thought about making him something.

Joanne Hmm. Like what?

Holly What about a cake? Everyone likes cakes, [4]*do they / don't they*?

Joanne Well, I do. OK, let's make him a cake. And we can put his name on it.

Holly Good idea. But we should start soon, otherwise we [5]*will / won't* have time.

Joanne OK. What do we need? [6]*I won't / I'll* go to the shops if you get the kitchen ready.

Holly Great. I'll do that. We will need sugar, chocolate, cream …

2 Circle T (True) or F (False) or DK (don't know) for the sentences below.

1 Steve is 21 years old tomorrow.   **T / F / DK**

2 Holly wants to bring him a present.   **T / F / DK**

3 Joanne wants to buy Steve some chocolates.   **T / F / DK**

4 Steve eats a lot of cakes.   **T / F / DK**

5 Joanne decides to go out to buy things.   **T / F / DK**

6 Holly will go with her to buy the ingredients for the cake. **T / F / DK**

3 Complete the dialogues with the sentences below.

1 Good idea. I'll make some sandwiches.   4 OK. I'll turn the DVD on.

2 OK. I'll get her some flowers.   5 OK. I'll email him now.

3 OK. I'll put on my shoes.   6 Yes. I'll make you one.

A Let's invite Pete.

B Let's have something to eat.

C Let's have some coffee.

D Let's get Mum a present.

E Let's watch a film.

F Let's go out.

Vocabulary and Communication

Food

1 Complete the words to talk about ways of cooking food.

1 I like the smell of freshly – b_ _ _ _ bread.
2 These vegetables aren't cooked – they are r_ _.
3 Put the cake in the oven, and b_ _ _ it for about 30 minutes.
4 The fish tastes very nice after it has been g_ _ _ _ _ _ for a few minutes.
5 I often have f_ _ _ _ eggs for breakfast.
6 The r _ _ _ _ chicken we had for lunch was delicious!

2 Circle 12 words for food and drink in the puzzle.

Y	S	P	I	N	A	C	H	B	C
H	A	I	T	E	E	O	F	R	H
A	U	N	Y	C	F	F	G	O	O
M	S	E	O	A	O	F	C	A	C
B	A	A	G	B	R	E	A	D	O
P	G	P	H	B	A	E	R	M	L
R	E	P	U	A	N	K	R	I	A
G	S	L	R	G	G	A	O	K	T
E	J	E	T	E	E	F	T	L	E
R	M	I	L	K	S	E	O	E	J

....
....
....
....
....
....
....
....
....
....
....
....

Talking about food

3 Complete the dialogue with the words below. Then listen and check.

hot	revolting	filling	nutritious	mild	fattening

Mark So what shall we order? How about a tasty curry?
Claire No, I don't like [1] .... and spicy food.
Mark We could order a [2] .... curry. A nice chicken curry with lots of yoghurt.
Claire No, yoghurt is too [3] .... I need to lose weight.
Mark OK. How about a salad? A fresh, [4] .... salad with lots of vitamins.
Claire No, that's too light. I want something a bit more [5] .... – otherwise I'll be hungry later.
Mark Right. Well, would you like some fish? Some fried fish?
Claire No! Fish is [6] .... I hate the taste.
Mark OK. Is there anything on the menu you would like?
Claire Yes – chocolate cake!

Grammar

will / won't for predictions

 Complete the sentences with *will* or *won't*.

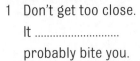

1 Don't get too close. It .... probably bite you.

2 Don't buy it now. It .... be cheaper on Monday.

3 We should buy it now – there .... be any left soon.

4 Don't be afraid. He .... bite you.

5 Number 13 definitely .... win the race now.

6 You shouldn't go in there – it .... be very cold.

7 Be careful, it .... be hot.

8 And number 13 .... surely win now.

 Complete the dialogues with the verbs below.

| will have | won't see | won't miss | will probably rain |
| will be (x2) | won't sleep | | |

1 **A** We're going on holiday tomorrow, so we ¹ .... you for a couple of weeks.

  B That's right. You're going to Greece, aren't you? I'm sure you ² .... beautiful weather.

  A I hope so. I'm tired of all this rain.

  B Yes, you ³ .... home – it ⁴ .... every day here!

  A Yes, probably!

2 **A** I'm really worried about my exam tomorrow.

  B Don't worry. You ⁵ .... fine. You're really clever.

  A Thanks but I'm nervous. I ⁶ .... tonight, I know.

  B Drink a cup of hot milk and you ⁷ .... asleep in minutes. I promise.

Grammar

Question tags (revision)

3 **Circle the correct question tag.**

1 You're Sandra, *isn't / aren't* you?

2 This is Paris, *isn't / wasn't* it?

3 I'm right, *aren't / was* I?

4 You didn't do your homework, *didn't / did* you?

5 It'll probably rain tomorrow, *isn't / won't* it?

6 The film wasn't very interesting, *was / wasn't* it?

7 She's going to London, *won't / isn't* she?

8 He doesn't like me, *does / is* he?

4 **Complete the question tags with the words below.**

is	will	didn't	wasn't	did	aren't	am	isn't	don't

1 It's cold today, ... it?

2 You like cooking, ... you?

3 Sushi isn't Chinese food, ... it?

4 Our teacher told us about the exam, ... he?

5 I'm not late, ... I?

6 We're going to be late, ... we?

7 You won't tell anyone, ... you?

8 She didn't apologise, ... she?

9 It was a brilliant match, ... it?

5 **Complete the dialogue with the correct question tag.**

Hannah Hey, Tom, you went to Greece last year, [1] ....?

Tom Yes, why?

Hannah I'm doing a homework project on another country's food.

Tom Oh you're a bit late, [2] ....? You're supposed to hand it in tomorrow!

Hannah Yes, I know … Anyway, Greek food. Tell me about some famous Greek food. Moussaka is Greek, [3] ....?

Tom Um, yes, but I don't think I ate any moussaka.

Hannah Oh. Well, the Greeks eat a lot of fresh fish, [4] ....? Did you eat any fish in Greece?

Tom Well, no, not really.

Hannah OK, well, how about your parents? They went with you, [5] ....?

Tom Yes, sure.

Hannah So, what did you all eat?

Tom Well, mostly, we ate food in the hotel. Chips, burgers, that kind of thing.

Hannah That's no good! I can't write about burgers, [6] ....?!

Skills

Reading

1 Read the first part of an article about 'slow food'. What do you think 'slow food' is?

> Do you often eat fast food? It is difficult not to as we are surrounded by it. You can see the same pizza and hamburger places in every city in the world. Every supermarket sells similar 'ready meals' which you just put in the microwave and eat after a few minutes. Fast food is everywhere. It is cheap and can be healthy and delicious, too.
>
> But what about 'slow food'? The idea of an alternative to fast food began in Italy in 1986. Now, the 'slow food' idea has spread to 150 different countries around the world.

2 Read the next part and check your ideas.

> Slow food is a return to basics. It is a type of cooking based on these principles:
>
> - The food must be made with local **ingredients** – not food imported from thousands of miles away. This helps local farmers keeps **traditions** alive.
>
> - The food must be made using **local**, traditional methods. So, no big factories or super-modern technology. The food must be made in the same way it was made hundreds of years ago.
>
> - Perhaps most importantly, the food must be healthy for the people who eat it, and also good for the people who make it.
>
> Is slow food really better than fast food? If it is healthy, yes. Food made from fresh, local ingredients is always going to be better than food made in a factory with lots of chemicals. And, if it helps local farmers keep in business, then it can't be bad.
>
> There are some disadvantages, though. There is a reason many of us eat fast food. It is because we don't have time to spend slowly preparing **delicious** food. Most of us have to study or work and we can't afford to spend hours chopping vegetables or baking bread.
>
> But, we shouldn't eat fast food all the time and learning to cook is a great skill. Sometimes, we need to learn how to be 'slow' again.

3 Match the words in bold in the article to these definitions.

1 ways of doing things that people have done for a long time: ....
2 very tasty: ....
3 the different foods which are part of one dish or meal: ....
4 from a small area of a country: ....

4 Read the article again and answer these questions.

1 What are the principles of 'slow food'? ....
2 How does 'slow food' help farmers? ....
3 Why don't more people eat 'slow food'? ....

Skills

Listening

  Listen to the dialogue and number the photos in the correct order.

 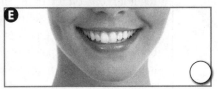

  Listen again and complete the sentences with the words below.

junk	responsibility	five	enjoy	diseases	athletes

1 We should eat .... portions of fruit and vegetables a day.
2 Some .... can be prevented if we eat more fruit and vegetables.
3 We shouldn't eat .... food for every meal.
4 It's also important to .... your food.
5 Most top .... don't eat bad food.
6 Parents have a lot of .... for what children learn about food.

Writing

7a Think about what you have eaten in the last five days. Make notes in the table below.

Healthy foods	Unhealthy foods

7b Now make notes on the questions below.

Do you:
1 eat alone or with other people?
2 cook your own food?
3 eat fresh food or prepared food?
4 eat what you enjoy?

8 Write a paragraph about what you have eaten in the last five days and how you usually eat.

Text work

1 **Read the article and match the photos to the correct places.**

How to greet people

There are many ways to greet people - you can shake hands, kiss, hug or just say *hello*.

In China, young people say 'hi' with a nod of their head. Older Chinese people might sometimes put their hands together, one on top of the other, in front of their throat and then nod. This technique is also used in Hong Kong.

In India and Thailand, you might see another way of greeting people. It is called the *namaste*. To do the *namaste*, you need to put the palms of your hands together in front of you and then nod or bend the upper part of your body a little. It is a polite way to make a guest feel welcome.

In Japan, there are many ways to bow when you meet another person. If you want to be formal, you need to do a little bow from the waist – that is, bend the upper part of your body forwards. At the same time, you need to keep the palms of your hands on the fronts of your legs and keep your feet together. In this culture, people don't shake hands.

In many Arab countries, like the United Arab Emirates, it is traditional for men to greet each other by rubbing their noses. This is a sign of close friendship. The nose is in the centre of the face and touching it is an important symbol of respect.

If you want to learn a difficult greeting, try a traditional Polish 'hello'. When you meet a friend, you kiss them on the cheek - not once or twice but three times. Everyone does it, but it is harder than it looks.

1 China   2 India and Thailand   3 Japan   4 Poland   5 the UAE

2 **Match the words (1–6) to the definitions (a–f).**

1	greet	a	to move your head up or down
2	nod	b	to move any part of your body to show what you're feeling
3	throat	c	to welcome someone
4	palm	d	the front of your neck
5	bow	e	the inside part of your hand
6	gesture	f	to bend your head or body forward

Vocabulary and Communication

1 Body movements

Complete the words about body movements.

1 He's f_ _ _ _ _ g his arms.

2 He has c_ _ _ _ _ d his legs.

3 He's n_ _ _ _ _ g his head.

4 He's s_ _ _ _ _ _ _ _ g his head.

5 She's s_ _ _ _ _ g her head.

6 She's w_ _ _ _ g goodbye.

careful!
7 The teacher is p_ _ _ _ _ _ g at the board.

8 They are s_ _ _ _ _ g hands.

Talking about body movements

32

2 Complete the sentences with the words below. Then listen and check.

> hands (x2)   head (x3)   finger   legs   arms

1 When I'm thinking about something, I sometimes scratch my ....
2 I point at things using my ....
3 When I agree, I nod my ....
4 I sometimes fold my .... when I'm angry.
5 When I disagree, I shake my ....
6 Sometimes, I cross my .... when I'm nervous.
7 I only wave my .... when I want to attract someone's attention.
8 When I meet someone for the first time, I usually shake .... with them.

Sounds right Units of speech

33

3 Listen and repeat the sentences from exercise 2. Write two lines // when you hear a pause in the sentence.

When I'm thinking about something // I sometimes scratch my head.

Grammar

could, might, may for speculation

1 Reorder the words to make sentences.

1 He's / Spanish, so / speaking / may / he / from Spain. / be /.

....

2 I don't / could / it / what language / be / know / it is, but / Japanese /.

....

3 Don't / rain / the / forget / might / umbrella – it / later /.

....

4 Please / him – he / be / phone / don't / may / asleep /.

....

5 I'm / be / sure / in / not / where / could / she / is – she / a meeting /.

....

6 Don't / that / bite / might / touch / dog – it / you /.

....

2 Rewrite the sentences to include the words in brackets.

1 If you run, it's possible you will be able to catch the train. (might)
   If you ....

2 It's possible she's feeling bad because she failed her exam. (may)
   She ....

3 He's very clever – it's possible he will become a doctor when he's older. (could)
   He's very ....

3 Complete the dialogues with the phrases below.

> could just be   could be busy   might be broken   may be right   may be having   might go up

Patient Hello Doctor, can you help me? I think my arm
¹ ....

Doctor Hmm. I don't think so. It ² .... a
small injury. What happened?

Pete We should buy the plane tickets now. The price
³ .... in a few days.

Sarah Yes, you ⁴ .... Where's your debit
card?

Paul Why hasn't Clara answered my email? Do you
think she hates me?

Mark No, no. She ⁵ .... , or she
⁶ .... some problems getting
online. But I'm sure she will answer soon.

Grammar

-ed vs -ing adjectives

4 Match the sentences to the correct pictures.

1 The children are boring.
2 The dog is frightening.
3 The children are bored.

4 The musician was amazed.
5 The dog is frightened.
6 The musician was amazing.

5 Match the beginnings and endings of each sentence.

1 The speaker was so boring
2 The speaker was so bored

  a that he fell asleep.
  b that I fell asleep.

3 I was really insulted
4 I was really insulting

  a when my brother said I looked fat.
  b when I said my brother looked fat.

5 I was very frightening
6 I was very frightened

  a when I watched that film.
  b when I wore my Halloween costume.

7 The actors were very excited –
8 The actors were very exciting –

  a we couldn't stop looking at them.
  b they couldn't stop giggling and laughing.

6 Complete the words with *ed* or *ing*.

1 I'm really worri .... about ....
2 I get very frighten................... when ....
3 I'm not very interest................... in ....
4 The most bor................... day of the week is ....
5 The most excit................... person I've ever met is ....
6 I usually feel tir................... when I ....
7 The most disappoint................... news I ever had was ....
8 The school subject I find most fascinat................... is ....

7 Now complete the sentences about yourself.

Skills

Reading

 1 **Read the article and tick (✓) the best title below.**

1 Should teenagers be allowed to wear what they want? ☐

2 Should teenagers go to school? ☐

3 Should teenagers be allowed to have their nose pierced? ☐

More and more teenagers are choosing to have piercings these days. Their parents often don't understand why and this can create problems at home. But who is right? Should adults accept that things might have changed from when they were young, or do mum and dad know best? We asked teenagers and parents what they thought.

THE TEENAGERS

All the girls in my school have earrings, that's no problem, but pierced noses are different. There aren't many students with pierced noses at my school so there's no pressure to have one. I think if someone wants to have one because they like the way it looks, they should be able to. They can always take it out when they're older if they don't like it any more.
Claire, 14

Our school doesn't allow students to have pierced noses so it doesn't really matter what parents think - the head teacher has already made the decision for us. I know some students think this is wrong and that they should be allowed to do what they want, but schools are full of rules. I don't see why there can't be one against pierced noses.
Karl, 15

THE PARENTS

When I was a teenager, I fought with my mum and dad because I wanted to get my ears pierced. I was disappointed I couldn't do it. In the end, I waited until I left home and went to university. I think I only did it to make my parents angry. If my children ask me if they can get their nose pierced, I'll have to think hard. I'll try to help them see why it's better to wait.
Mark, 45

I don't mind if my children want to get their noses pierced. It's a fashion and like most fashions, it really doesn't matter. But I would make sure they go somewhere official, to ensure it's hygienic. If they don't like it in the future, they can just take the studs out. What's the harm?
Dawn, 34

---

 2 **Read the article again and write the name of the correct person.**

Who ....

1 thinks piercing is not an important issue? ....

2 pierced their ears to annoy their mum and dad? ....

4 doesn't feel under any pressure to get a nose stud? ....

4 would prefer their children to wait before making a decision about getting a nose stud?

....

5 thinks teenagers should be able to look the way they want to? ....

Skills

Listening

34

3 Listen to a talk about body language and number the pictures in the correct order.

4 Match the sentence halves.

1 When you stand close to someone,
2 If you don't like someone,
3 If your arms are folded,
4 If someone touches their face,
5 When someone's tapping their feet

a you don't look at them.
b you might be angry.
c they may want to get away.
d it might mean that you like them.
e they could be lying.

Writing

5 Read part of an email from a friend. What is the problem?

I'm really enjoying going to the gym. It keeps my body healthy and I like meeting other people there. I think it's really important to keep yourself fit. The problem is, I have a lot of exams next month. My parents say I should spend more time at home studying.
What do you think?

6 You are going to reply to your friend, but first put these paragraphs in order.

A Suggest saying to the parents that he/she might do better in the exams if he/she could go to the gym. Suggest making a timetable with both study and exercise included. ☐

B Say thanks for the email. Say that you would like to start going to the gym one day. ☐

C Say it's important not to stop going to the gym. It could be difficult to go back if you stop going now! ☐

7 Write a reply in 100 words, using the three paragraphs from exercise 6. Remember to use informal, friendly language!

Learning to learn (Units 7 and 8)

Vocabulary maps

Vocabulary maps are a useful way to record words.

There are two main things that you can do with vocabulary maps. One is to record groups of words according to topic. The other thing you can do is record words which go together. Recording new vocabulary like this in your notebook will help you remember it, and it looks good, too!

1 **Write the words below in the correct vocabulary map. Use a dictionary to help you.**

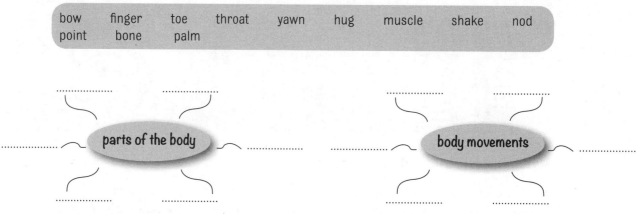

bow   finger   toe   throat   yawn   hug   muscle   shake   nod
point   bone   palm

parts of the body

body movements

Collocations

Words which go together are called collocations. They can be verb + noun collocations or adjective + preposition collocations

2 **Complete these collocations with the words and phrases below.**

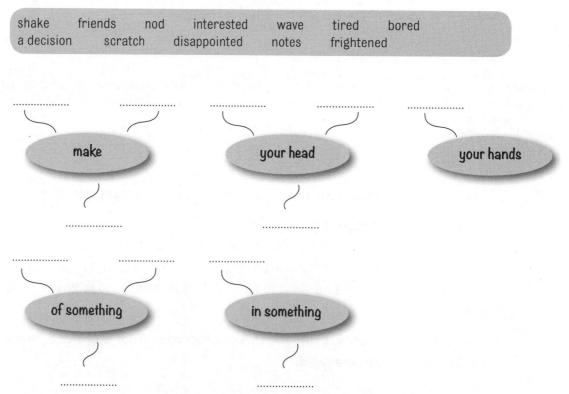

shake   friends   nod   interested   wave   tired   bored
a decision   scratch   disappointed   notes   frightened

make

your head

your hands

of something

in something

Exam skills 4

Speaking

1 Look at these photos of people greeting each other. Choose one of the photos and make notes about what you can see in the table.

Who the people are	
How they are feeling	
What they are doing	

2 Work in pairs. Describe your photo to your partner in one minute.

Tip Try to time yourself speaking with a watch (or your phone). Stop speaking when the time is up.

In this photo, the people are …

They could be …

I think they might be …

3 The photos above show different people meeting. Make notes on the questions below.

1 When you meet a friend, do you shake hands, or hug them?
2 Do you like meeting new people?
3 How do you feel when you meet someone new?
4 What things do you prefer to talk about when you meet someone new?

4 Now discuss the questions with a friend for two minutes.

Dialogue work

35

1 Complete the dialogue with the phrases below.
Then listen and check.

> picture   comedy   awards   characters   actor   story

Bill   What did you think of the film?

Susan   I'm not sure. The ¹..................... was good, but the acting was terrible.

Bill   No way! I thought the acting was great.

Susan   You must be joking. They just acted stupid all the time.

Bill   Well, it was a ²..................... . They were stupid ³..................... . You know the main character, Jack? Well the ⁴..................... who played him used to play serious roles.

Susan   Really? I can't imagine him being serious.

Bill   Yes, he has been in some of the best films ever made. He's won lots of ⁵..................... . So it was good to see him playing such a different part.

Susan   I've never seen him in anything else.

Bill   We can watch one of his more serious films next time. One of them won Best ⁶..................... at the Oscars.

Susan   OK, I'll try and buy that one.

Bill   Don't bother, I've got it at home. Why don't you come round and watch it with me?

Susan   Great – I'd like that.

2 Read the sentences and circle T (True) or F (False).

1 Susan didn't like the acting in the film.   T / F
2 Bill agrees with her.   T / F
3 The main actor is usually in comedy films.   T / F
4 Susan has never seen this actor's other films.   T / F
5 Bill doesn't have any of his films.   T / F
6 Susan doesn't want to watch the film with Bill.   T / F

3 Match the questions and the answers.

1 Who's your favourite singer?   a I used to love banana sandwiches!
2 What's your favourite type of film?   b Will Ferrell, definitely!
3 Who's your favourite actor?   c It's Adele.
4 What was your favourite food when   d Mushroom pizza – but I used to hate it!
   you were a kid?   e I usually watch comedies.
5 What's your favourite food now?

Vocabulary and Communication

Awards shows

 1 Complete the sentences with the words below.

best picture   best actress   best solo female artist   best animated film   best actor
best single   best group   best solo male artist   best album

1 And the award for

....

goes to Leonardo di Caprio.

2 And the award for

....

goes to Bruno Mars.

3 And the award for

....

goes to Jesse J.

4 And the award for

....

goes to *Frozen*.

5 And the award for

....

goes to Sandra Bullock.

6 And the award for

....

goes to One Direction.

7 And the award for

....

goes to *Dear Darlin'* by
Olly Murs.

8 And the award for

....

goes to *The Blessed Unrest*.

9 And the award for

....

goes to *Gravity*.

Sounds right Questions with *would*

 2 Listen and circle the stressed words.

1 Who would you like to win the award for best actor or actress?
2 Which album or single would you like to win?
3 Which film would you choose for best picture?
4 Who would you choose for best solo male or female artist?

Grammar

used to

1 **Complete the sentences with *used to* or *use to*.**

1 My parents .... live in Tokyo.
2 I didn't .... like vegetables.
3 We .... play football every Saturday afternoon.
4 He didn't .... watch a lot of TV.
5 I didn't .... speak to my neighbours.
6 Did your brother .... play in a band?

2 **Complete the sentences with the correct form of (*not*) *used to* and the verbs in brackets.**

1 I .... French, but now I can say a lot of things. (speak)
2 We .... to the park every weekend, but now it's closed for the winter. (go)
3 I .... coffee, but now I drink it every morning. (like)
4 My sister .... a job, but now she's a bank manager. (have)
5 I .... with my sister a lot, but now we're good friends. (argue)
6 She .... blonde hair, but now she's changed it to dark brown. (have)

3 **Read about Sally and complete the gaps with the correct form of *used to*.**

I ¹ .... go to the cinema at least once a week – sometimes twice! I loved going with friends and watching the latest blockbuster. Now, I've changed completely. I still watch a lot of films, but I watch them on TV or on my computer at home. I ² .... have a computer but now I have a very good one and I can download any film or TV show I want. It ³ .... be illegal to download films but now you can. I ⁴ .... like being at home, but now I love it!

4 **Write questions about Sally using *used to*.**

1 Sally – go to the cinema a lot? (Yes, she did.)

....

2 she – go the cinema with friends or alone? (With friends.)

....

3 she – like staying at home? (No, she didn't.)

....

4 she – have a computer? (No, she didn't.)

....

Grammar

Gerunds after prepositions

5 **Circle the correct words.**

1 I invited Sara to the cinema, but she said she's not interested *at / in* going.
2 I'm not very good *at / on* cooking.
3 The new *Iron Man* film is coming out soon – I'm looking forward *into / to* it.
4 I didn't use to like horror films, but now I'm really keen *on / of* them.
5 She loves sci-fi movies at the moment – she's really *into / in* them.

6 **Complete the sentences with a preposition and the correct form of the verb in brackets.**

1 I'm thinking .... (buy) a new laptop.
2 Are you looking forward .... (see) the new film?
3 I was enjoying the party, but my friend insisted .... (leave).
4 He's not very good .... (tell) jokes.
5 She's really bad .... (explain) things clearly.
6 Sorry, I'm not interested .... (listen) to your problems.

7 **Use the words below and write captions for each picture.**

1 they – look forward – leave

....

2 she – not interest – look at cars

....

3 their father – not very good – cook

....

4 he – think – buy – a new car

....

Skills

Reading

1 Read the article quickly and tick (✓) the title that best describes it.

1 The article is about three famous people. ☐

2 The article is about three people talking about being famous. ☐

3 The article is about three people who want to be famous. ☐

Fame!

Alison

I've always dreamed ¹ *to / of* being famous. It would be great to be in a successful band. I could travel the world and see all those places that I've wanted to visit. And you wouldn't have to organise anything, someone would do it all for you. I'd only fly first class and stay in five-star hotels. I'd also get to meet lots of interesting people and hang out with other famous people. It must be great never having to worry about money and buying everything you want. Of course, I would insist ² *to / on* making things better for other people, too. So, I would give a lot of money to charity.

Jonathan

I'd be really bad ³ *in / at* being famous. The money would be OK, but I'd hate to lose my privacy. Imagine never being able to go anywhere without hundreds of journalists following you everywhere. It would be a nightmare. These days, there are far too many people who are famous ⁴ *for / in* doing nothing. I blame reality TV and talent shows. They take ordinary people and try to make them special. They're not special. They're just ordinary like you and me.

Lara

I'd like to be respected by people who respect me. If this makes me famous, then that's great but if it doesn't, it's no big problem. I'm really keen ⁵ *on / in* writing poetry. I'm a member of a writing group and sometimes we read out our poems to each other. It's a great feeling when people hear your poems and are interested ⁶ *on / in* them. I've even had some poems printed in our local newspaper. That was a great experience. Not many people become famous writing poems so I don't expect much. It would be nice to earn a living writing poetry. I'd be happy with that.

2 Read the article again and circle the correct prepositions.

3 Read the sentences and circle T (True) or F (False).

1	Alison doesn't want to be famous.	**T / F**
2	She would like to be rich and travel everywhere.	**T / F**
3	Jonathan thinks that a lot of famous people are not special.	**T / F**
4	He thinks being famous would be very nice.	**T / F**
5	Lara isn't interested in becoming famous.	**T / F**
6	She doesn't want to continue writing.	**T / F**

Skills

Listening

 HAVE YOU GOT TALENT? DO YOU WANT TO BE FAMOUS?
We're looking for the stars of tomorrow!

Just come along to our auditions on Saturday morning in the Town Hall at 3 o'clock. You will be seen by our famous TV judges. You could have the chance to appear on our TV show, and go on to become one of the most famous people in the country!

37

4 **Read the poster and listen to the dialogue. Match the sentence halves.**

1 Max and Polly are both going to
2 Polly is going to
3 Max is going to

a go with a dog.
b sing and play guitar.
c enter the talent contest.

38

5 **Listen again. Read the sentences and circle T (True) or F (False).**

1 Polly can't sing or play an instrument.   **T / F**
2 Polly's dog can't walk or jump.   **T / F**
3 Polly's dog is very good at juggling.   **T / F**
4 Max's band was not very popular.   **T / F**
5 He will go with his band to the talent contest.   **T / F**

Writing

6 **Read the review of Polly and Spot's performance. Is it mostly positive or mostly negative? Circle the words which helped you decide.**

Polly and her dog Spot gave a great performance – the judges loved them. One of the judges is a big fan of dogs, so Polly chose the right act! Spot really is a talented dog. The way he walked on two legs was amazing. He was so cute! But the highlight of the show was when he jumped through some hoops that were on fire. It was incredible. The judges were on their feet, clapping. Polly and Spot will probably appear in the TV show, so if you get the chance, I highly recommend that you watch them.

7 **Plan a review of something you liked. Follow the instructions below.**

1 Choose something you enjoyed: a film, a TV show, a book, a concert, etc.
2 Make notes on the reasons you enjoyed it.
3 Think of some positive words and phrases you can use to describe it.
4 Would you recommend it to someone else? Why?

8 **Write your review in about 150 words. Give it to your teacher to read.**

Text work

1 Read the blog quickly. Number the photos in the order they are mentioned.

FAMOUS COLLECTORS!!

A

C

B

D

E

Many people collect things from their favourite celebrities or film stars: photos, DVDs, items of clothing etc. But what about celebrities? What kinds of thing do they collect?

Most celebrities have a lot of money to spend, so a lot of famous people have large art collections. For example, Brad Pitt has been collecting art made from metal for many years and Christina Aguilera has spent a lot of money on famous pieces of graffiti. Usain Bolt, one of the fastest people in the world, loves collecting cars. He owns BMWs, Ferraris, and even a Formula 1 race car. George Clooney has a huge motorbike collection. He rides different bikes all over the world and Hollywood actor John Travolta has been collecting aeroplanes for years. He has a huge Boeing 707 and is a certified pilot. He even has his own runway so he can step out of his front door and onto an airplane.

However, some film stars have more unusual interests. Tom Hanks has a passion for typewriters. He has more than 200, and says he loves the sound they make as he hits the keys!

2 Circle T (True) or F (False) or DK (don't know) for the sentences below.

1 Brad Pitt has been collecting metal for many years.   **T / F / DK**

2 Usain Bolt is one of a number of celebrities who collects vehicles.   **T / F / DK**

3 George Clooney puts his motorbikes in a garage and never uses them.   **T / F / DK**

4 John Travolta collects planes but he can't fly them.   **T / F / DK**

5 Tom Hanks has been collecting typewriters for 20 years.   **T / F / DK**

Vocabulary and Communication

Hobbies and pastimes

1 Complete the words about hobbies and pastimes.

1 I love c _ _ _ _ _ _. I enjoy trying out new recipes.

2 When I was young, I used to enjoy playing b_ _ _ _ games. My grandmother taught me how to play a game called Monopoly.

3 My hobby is m_ _ _ _ _ _ things. There's nothing I love more than getting something that's broken, and repairing it.

4 In my spare time, I do a lot of p_ _ _ _ _ _ _ _ _. Nothing serious – but I love taking photos of flowers, animals and sunsets.

5 My grandfather does a lot of g_ _ _ _ _ _ _ _ now that he's retired. He spends a lot of time just looking after his flowers and vegetables.

6 One of the best hobbies is playing a musical i_ _ _ _ _ _ _ _ _. I play the guitar, and it's a great way to relax.

7 I used to like making m_ _ _ _ _ when I was a boy. I used to make little planes and ships.

8 I like c_ _ _ _ _ _ _ _ things. At the moment, I have 300 different postcards from different countries around the world. I ask people to send me them whenever they travel.

9 A lot of people enjoy playing c_ _ _ _ _ _ _ games in their spare time.

2 Write four hobbies that people you know like doing.

Example: ..My brother likes playing computer games...

1 ....

2 ....

3 ....

4 ....

Talking about hobbies

3 Listen to the dialogue. Which hobbies are mentioned? Tick (✓) the correct pictures.

Sounds right Question stress

4 Listen and repeat the questions from exercise 3. Circle the stressed words.

1 How long have you been learning that?

2 How long have you been doing that?

3 How long have you been gardening?

Grammar

Present perfect continuous

1 Match the sentences to the correct pictures.

1 He's been sleeping all night.
2 He's been running.

3 He's been learning the piano for years.
4 He's been studying all night.

2 Complete the sentences with the Present perfect continuous of the verbs in brackets.

1 I .... (wait) here since 11.30, and there's still no sign of John.
2 Paul .... (watch) TV since he woke up this morning. Doesn't he do anything all day?
3 I'm not very good at the piano, although I .... (take) lessons for two years now.
4 I hope you like the food tonight – I .... (cook) the whole afternoon!
5 Susan can't come to school today – she .... (feel) ill all weekend.
6 I'm exhausted – I .... (run) for more than an hour!
7 Don't your eyes hurt? You .... (work) in front of that computer for hours.
8 Mark and Karen are still at the library – they .... (study) there all morning.

3 Use the words below and write sentences in the Present perfect continuous.

1 How long – you – learn – Spanish?

....

2 I – look – my keys all morning. I can't find them.

....

3 She – cook – food – all afternoon for the party.

....

4 I – write – emails since 3 o'clock.

....

5 I – read – this book for three months now.

....

6 How long – he – play – tennis?

....

Grammar

Embedded questions

4 Circle the correct words.

How much is it?

1 She doesn't know how much *is it* / *it is.*

What's her name?

2 He wants to know what *her name is* / *is her name.*

Where am I?

3 He doesn't know where *is he* / *he is.*

How old are you?

4 The police officer wants to know how old *is he* / *he is.*

How can we get out?

5 They don't know how *can they* / *they can* get out.

What time is it going to finish?

6 He's wondering what time *it is* / *is it* going to finish.

5 Reorder the words below to write sentences.

1 Do / know / you / this / how much / costs / ?

....

2 know / what / time / it / is / you / Do / ?

....

3 I / know / shop / when / don't / the / opens / .

....

4 I'd / to / he / know / like / where / lives / .

....

6 Complete the answers.

1 **A** What's the time?
  B Sorry, I don't know what time ....
  ....

2 **A** How many people are in the room?
  B I'm afraid I don't know how ....
  ....

3 **A** When does the train arrive?
  B I have no idea when ....
  ....

4 **A** How much does it cost?
  B Sorry, I'm not sure how ....
  ....

Skills

Reading

1 Read the article quickly and tick (✓) the title that best describes it.

1 The Rubbish Museum ☐
2 The World's Most Popular Museum ☐
3 The World's Worst Museum ☐

Have you ever been to a museum and thought that it was a load of rubbish? Well, most people who go to the Trash Museum in Hartford, USA, have exactly the same opinion! This museum features art works made out of recycled rubbish, and you can also take part in workshops to create your own 'rubbish art'!

The exhibition of rubbish covers 6,500 square feet. You can follow the history of rubbish from pre-historic times to today. There is also a lot of useful information about how rubbish can be re-used. The museum has a serious message about how much we waste and the problems this causes to the environment. There is even a 'trash souvenir shop' where you can buy clothes and other beautiful objects made from recycled materials.

2 Read the sentences and circle T (True) or F (False) or DK (don't know).

1 The museum is for works of art made from recycled rubbish. **T / F / DK**
2 You can create your own work of art in the museum. **T / F / DK**
3 The museum is owned by two brothers. **T / F / DK**
4 The museum just shows people what modern rubbish is like. **T / F / DK**
5 The museum has a special area for families. **T / F / DK**

3 Find words in the text for the definitions below.

1 used again ....
2 spreads over something ....
3 to not use something properly ....
4 an object you buy to remind you of a place or a person ....

Skills

Listening

4 Listen to two people talking about a collection. What does Martin collect? Tick (✓) the correct photo.

5 Listen again and complete each sentence with one word.

1 Sarah got a letter from her friend in ....

2 Sarah didn't know that Martin collects ....

3 Sarah thinks that almost no-one writes .... these days.

4 Max started after his .... showed him his collection.

5 Max's collection is mostly from .... countries.

6 Max says that they have lots of different ....

7 He only collects .... ones.

8 He has four ....

Reading and writing

6 Complete this introduction to stamp collecting with the phrases below.

is interesting because   it's a good hobby because   another advantage is
a good thing to do   you can start

I started stamp collecting when I was about 12 years old. [1] .... you don't need a lot of money. [2] .... by collecting used stamps – just take the stamps off real letters and postcards that people have sent.

[3] .... is to check your own post. Of course, you will probably find lots of your own country's stamps at the beginning, but that's OK – it's a start!

Then, it's easy to ask your family and friends to give you letters or postcards that they receive. Older relatives might have very old postcards with stamps which are very rare.

Stamp collecting [4] .... you can learn a lot about the different countries around the world. Most stamps have very beautiful, interesting designs. And [5] .... that they can be worth a lot of money in the future!

7 Plan to write about a hobby you like or know about. Follow the instructions below.

1 Decide what hobby you want to write about.

2 How can people start doing this hobby?

3 How can people continue doing it?

4 Why is it interesting?

8 Write about the hobby in 100 words. Use phrases from exercise 5 and your notes from exercise 6.

Learning to learn (Units 9 and 10)

Collocations (2)

Collocations are words which go together with other words. For example, *take a photo* is a collocation. It uses the verb *take* + the noun *photo*. We don't say ~~do a photo~~ or ~~make a photo~~. Collocations are important because they help us speak and write more naturally.

Tip When you read in English, pay attention to any collocations you see. Record them in a notebook and try to use them.

1 **Look at these sentences and the collocations in bold. Match them to the types of word below.**

1 James collects stamps. When he wants to find out more information about them, he **does research** on the internet.
2 He is a **highly intelligent** man. He has four degrees and teaches at University.
3 She was very tired and fell into a **deep sleep**. She woke up at noon the next day.
4 **Heavy rain** is forecast for tomorrow. We won't be able to go out.
5 If you're busy, why don't you **take a break**?
6 It was a **bitterly cold** winter. The temperature was - 40 degrees.

a verb + noun   .... , ...
b adjective + noun   .... , ...
c adverb + adjective   .... , ...

2 **Some verbs (like *make*, *do* and *have*) are very common in collocations. Circle the correct verb in these sentences.**

1 It's easier to *make / have / do* friends with people who have the same hobbies as you.
2 My sister is *making / having / doing* a baby next month!
3 I haven't got any hobbies. I like to sit around at home *making / having / doing* nothing.
4 I'm really bad at *making / having / doing* decisions – it takes me hours to think of what to do.
5 We *made / had / did* a really good time on holiday last year.

3 **Look at the verbs in bold in the story below. Which nouns do they go with?**

My stupid day

I had a terrible morning. Last night, I [1] **did** my homework, [2] **had** a shower and went to bed early because I was [3] **taking** an exam at 9 o'clock in the morning. I woke up early, [4] **had** a coffee and decided to [5] **take** the bus instead of walking to school. Unfortunately, I [6] **made** a terrible mistake. I left my purse at home. All I had was my debit card, and of course, on the bus you can't [7] **pay** by card. So, I asked a nice woman to [8] **do** me a favour. I explained that I was taking an important exam and I needed to get to school quickly. Luckily, the woman was really kind and gave me some money for the bus.

1 have a   ....
2 pay by   ....
3 do someone a ....
4 have a   ....

5 make a   ....
6 take an   ....
7 do your   ....
8 take the   ....

Exam skills 5

Speaking and reading

1 **Answer these questions.**

1 Do you like collecting things?
2 What do you think about people who spend lot of money on collecting things?
3 Look at the title of the article and the photo below. What do you think the article will be about?

2 **Read the article and choose the correct word (A, B, C or D) for each space.**

Tip Make sure you look around the gap to see what other words are in the sentence. Pay attention to collocations.

Would you like to drive like James Bond?

JAMES BOND has been thrilling movie audiences [1] .... 1962. When people think of these films, they [2] .... think of the incredible action scenes, especially the exciting car chases.

Well, now, you could be the owner [3] .... a real James Bond car! The world's largest collection of cars from the James Bond movies is [4] .... sale. A multi-millionaire from the USA bought most of the cars in

2011. Michael Dezer [5] .... a lot of time and money building his collection of Bond cars until he reached 59 vehicles.

He [6] .... his cars on display at a museum in Miami, Florida, but then [7] .... the decision to sell his collection. He wants to [8] .... money by selling the collection for an amazing £20 million.

The cars include six Aston Martins (James Bond's favourite vehicle), as well as a car [9] .... can travel underwater.

1	**A** for	**B** by	**C** at	**D** since
2	**A** mainly	**B** greatly	**C** totally	**D** hugely
3	**A** in	**B** of	**C** at	**D** to
4	**A** up	**B** to	**C** for	**D** from
5	**A** made	**B** spent	**C** did	**D** took
6	**A** put	**B** did	**C** had	**D** made
7	**A** did	**B** made	**C** had	**D** gave
8	**A** do	**B** put	**C** spend	**D** make
9	**A** what	**B** where	**C** which	**D** who

Dialogue work

43

1 Circle the correct words to complete the sentences. Then listen and check.

Luca What's the matter? You look a bit down.

Adam Yes, I've got a problem.

Luca Do you want to talk about it?

Adam Yes, but I *¹say / said* I wouldn't tell anyone.

Luca Who did you say that to?

Adam My brother. I'm going to tell you anyway, because I need some advice. Jim's been acting very strangely lately. A few days ago I went into his room to get a CD. He'd borrowed it from me but he's terrible at

giving things back! While I was looking for the CD I found a box full of mobile phones. I'm sure they were stolen. Just then, Jim came into the room. He was really angry and *²ask / asked* me *³what / that* I was doing there. I asked *⁴him / to him* where he'd got the phones from and he *⁵told / told me* it was none of my business. He warned *⁶me / to me* that if I *⁷spoke / said* about it to anyone, he would run away from home. Now I don't know what to do. Should I tell my parents? He's obviously in trouble, and I want to help him, but I don't want him to run away!

Luca Well, if I were you, I'd definitely tell someone. Maybe not your parents, though, but someone else, a teacher perhaps, or another adult who you trust.

2 Answer the questions.

1 What does Luca want Adam to do about his problem? ....

2 Who doesn't want Adam to tell anyone? ....

3 Why did Adam decide to tell Luca? ....

4 What did Adam ask his brother? ....

5 What is Adam afraid will happen, if he tells anyone? ....

6 What does Luca tell Adam to do? ....

3 Match the questions and the answers.

1 What's the matter? Is there something wrong?   a No. I promise I won't.

2 You won't tell anyone, will you?   b If I were you, I'd tell a teacher.

3 Your brother's been acting strangely, hasn't he?   c Yes, sometimes.

4 Should I tell someone?   d Yes, I've got a problem.

5 You're good at solving problems, aren't you?   e Yes. He's not usually like this.

Vocabulary and Communication

Personality adjectives

1 Circle the correct adjective to describe the people in the pictures.

1 *brave / unadventurous*   2 *considerate / selfish*   3 *outgoing / shy*   4 *sensible / sensitive*

2 Read the definitions and complete the words.

1 someone who is kind and helpful: c_ _ _ _ _ _ _ _ _ _
2 someone who accepts people who have different ideas or feelings from their own: t_ _ _ _ _ _ _
3 someone who is always happy and thinks good things will happen: p_ _ _ _ _ _ _
4 someone who makes good decisions: s_ _ _ _ _ _ _
5 someone who behaves in a stupid way: s_ _ _ _
6 someone who is frightened: s_ _ _ _ _
7 someone who usually thinks bad things will happen: n_ _ _ _ _ _ _

Describing people

3 Complete the dialogue with the words below. Then listen and check.

> sensitive   tolerant   shy   considerate   positive

Sue   Mark is fantastic!

Katie Yeah … But he's usually really ¹..................... . He doesn't like anyone looking at him. He prefers to be in the background. But, he likes you!

Sue   I thought he was really ²..................... . He was really cheerful, and looking for the good points in everything.

Katie Yeah, not like Sarah. She's so negative. I didn't like her at all.

Sue   Oh, I like Sarah. She can be negative, but she cares about other people and wants to help them. So, she's really ³..................... . She's always very ⁴..................... – she doesn't judge people. But she's also very ⁵..................... – her feelings get hurt very easily.

Sounds right Reporting direct speech

4 Listen and repeat the direct and reported speech.

1a 'Mark is fantastic!'

b She said that Mark was fantastic.

2a 'She's so negative. I didn't like her at all.'

b He said that she was so negative, and he didn't like her at all.

Grammar

Reported speech

1 Write the reported speech for the sentences below. Use the correct form of *say*.

1 **Paula:** I'm not interested in horror films.
2 **Ivan:** I can't come to the party.
3 **Mary:** I'm going away.
4 **John:** I'll be late.
5 **Suzy:** There has been a terrible traffic jam.

1 *Paula said she wasn't interested in horror films.*
2 ....
3 ....
4 ....
5 ....

2 Circle the words to complete the sentences.

1 I *said / told* that I wasn't feeling very well.
2 Steve *said / told* that he wanted to ask me a question.
3 We *said / told* the teacher that we had forgotten our homework.
4 Mr Brown *said / told* us not to be so noisy.
5 He *said / told* me to come inside.
6 My mother *said / told* she wouldn't be home until 7 o'clock.

3 Write the sentences in reported speech. Use the words in brackets.

Mrs. Brown, we've got a present for you!

Mike, I'm going to move to Canada.

1 .... (the children; say)

....

2 .... (Jenny; Mike; tell)

....

Anna has had a baby boy!

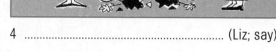

I will buy you a new one.

3 .... (Sam; his mother; tell)

....

4 .... (Liz; say)

....

Grammar

Reported questions

4 Read the sentences and write the original questions in the speech bubbles.

He asked her how long she had been a singer.

He asked them if they were going to have a shower.

He asked him why he hadn't done his homework.

She asked them if they were having a good time.

5 Match the reported questions with the answers.

1 She asked me where I was going.	a I told her that my dad was working there.
2 Then she asked me why I was going there.	b I told her I would stay two weeks.
3 She asked me how I was going to get there.	c 'Wait and see!' I said.
4 She asked me how long I was going to stay.	d I said I was going alone.
5 Then she asked me who I was going with.	e I said 'London.'
6 Finally, she asked me what I would buy her.	f I said I was going by plane.

6 Your friend, Sara, asks you these questions. Write the reported questions.

1 How are you?
She asked me how I was.

2 Do you want to come to the cinema?

3 Have you seen *Iron Man 4?*

4 How much are the tickets?

5 Where can we get a pizza?

6 What time do you have to go back home?

Skills

Reading

1 Tick (✓) the best definition of the word 'bullying'. Then read the article below.

1 to fight someone and win ☐

2 to hurt someone bigger and more powerful than you ☐

3 to hurt or frighten someone who you think is smaller or weaker than you ☐

BULLYING IN THE 21ST CENTURY

Jenna, 14, used to be bullied. She believes that most people are bullied at some point and they should talk about their experiences. They should never keep it a secret.

Jenna says that many people who are bullied suffer alone. For her, it started online when some people started sending very unpleasant messages to her email address. These were always anonymous – Jenna never knew who the messages came from. But they didn't stop. People called her names and teased her because of the way she looked.

Jenna told us that every time she tried to block the bullies from sending her messages, they would start again with a different name. She doesn't know for sure who was sending the messages, but she said that it was probably two or three other girls at her school.

After a few months, Jenna became ill because she was so upset. She felt that she had no friends, and that everyone hated her. She started missing lessons at school, and doing badly in exams. But luckily, she was able to talk to just one special person in her family about it – her 80-year-old grandmother, Muriel. Even though Muriel didn't know anything about the internet, she was able to tell Jenna that bullies were always the same, at all stages of life.

The best thing to do, said Muriel, was to completely ignore the bullies. Laugh at them, and understand that really they are the ones who are small and weak.

Jenna says that talking with her grandmother really helped solve the problem. She felt better about herself and didn't feel so alone.

Muriel believes that nobody deserves to be bullied. But if you don't tell anyone what is going on, nobody will know that you need help.

2 Who do you think said the following: Jenna or Muriel? Write the correct name below.

1 'I don't have any friends.' ....

2 'Don't pay attention to the bullies.' ....

3 'I think I know who sent the messages.' ....

4 'Bullies were just the same when I was your age.' ....

5 'I started to feel sick, and I didn't want to go to school.' ....

6 'If you feel bad, talk to someone about it.' ....

Skills

Listening

3 Listen to the interview. What is 'TAB'?

....

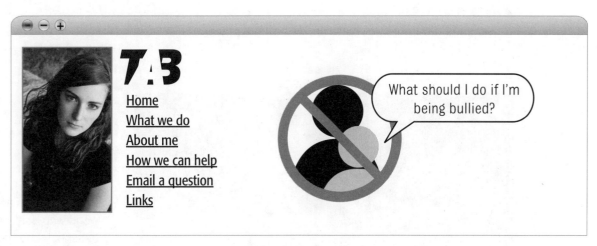

4 Listen again. Then answer the questions below.

1 When did Jenna start her website?

....

2 Why don't most people tell anyone they are being bullied?

....

3 What happened when she was bullied at her first school?

....

4 Who did she talk to at her new school?

....

5 What did she do with her new friends?

....

6 Why did other school councils ask her to help them?

....

Writing

5 Think of a time when you had a problem and someone gave you advice. Make notes on the questions below.

1 How old were you at the time?
2 What was the problem?
3 How did you feel?
4 Who gave you the advice?
5 What did they say to you?
6 Was the advice good or not?

6 Write a paragraph about the problem and the advice you got. Use reported speech to write about what the person who gave you the advice said.

UNIT 12 It's just not fair!

Text work

1 Read the article quickly and tick (✓) the title that best describes it.

1 How to be rich and famous. ☐

2 Why are some people so unhappy? ☐

3 We should think about our lives in a different way. ☐

1 A famous man once said 'life is not fair'. Now, who was this man? A poet, a street cleaner? No, it was actually one of the world's most famous billionaires, Bill Gates. You might feel this is a strange thing to say, if you are a huge businessman, a computer genius, and used to be the owner of Microsoft. But actually, he wanted to give some good advice to teenagers.

2 According to Bill Gates, the first and most important thing to learn is that life really is unfair! The world is not a nice, lovely place where all our dreams come true. Bad things happen, too. We might have parents who tell us what to do, or teachers who give us annoying homework, or we might even work in a boring job, doing things we don't want to do, for little money. The real world is not like TV. Very few people in real life want to help us. And really, the world is a difficult and scary place.

3 Why did Bill Gates say these things? The reason is simple. He wanted to make us work harder. Because when we understand that the world doesn't owe us anything, it makes us try more, and realise that we should be happy for what we have.

4 So we hate our homework? We shouldn't. There are millions of kids around the world who don't even go to school, and have no lessons. We are the lucky ones. So we hate our job making burgers in a bad restaurant? No problem – our grandparents would have been very happy if they had had a job like that! So our teachers or parents are mean and tell us what to do? Well, be careful! One day, you might have a boss who is 1,000 times worse!

5 What Bill Gates wanted to say was that we should be grateful for what we have. Yes, it's true that life is not fair. Things can be tough, but they could also be a lot worse. And there are many people in the world who would love to have the life that you have. So make the most of it!

2 Read the article again. Match the summaries below to the correct paragraph. Write 1-5.

a We can't always be happy and successful. ☐

b We are luckier than we think. ☐

c A successful person wanted to give some advice to younger people. ☐

d Be happy for what you have. ☐

e If we realise that life isn't fair, then we might fight harder for what we want. ☐

Vocabulary and Communication

Work places

1 Complete the crossword about work places.

Across

1 A place where goods are kept before they go into shops.
5 A place where products are made.
6 A place where an aerobics teacher works.
7 A place where minerals are dug out of the ground.

Down

2 A place where scientists experiment.
3 A place where people work with computers, phones, etc.
4 A place where criminals go after a trial.
5 A place where products are grown.

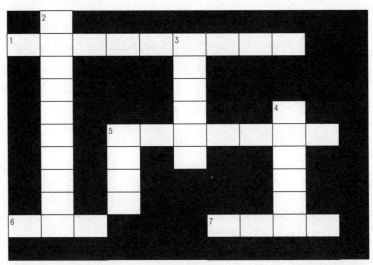

Talking about work and work places

 2 Listen and complete the dialogue.

Alan   What job would you like to do, Lizzie?

Lizzie   Well, my mum wants me to be a scientist, or a lawyer. But I would really hate to work in a ¹........................ , or a ²........................ , or anything like that. If I was a farmer, I could be outdoors every day. I could grow things. It would be great.

Alan   Do you think so? I wouldn't like to be outside every day. If it rained, it would be horrible!

Lizzie   OK. What job would you like?

Alan   Well, I would be happy if I had a nice, normal job. So, if I worked in an ³........................ , that would be OK.

Lizzie   Really? That's not so exciting.

Alan   I know. But it's better than working down a ⁴........................ or in a ⁵........................ .

Sounds right *If* clauses

3 Listen and practise saying the sentences.

1 If I was a farmer, I could be outdoors every day.
2 If it rained, it would be horrible!
3 I would be happy if I had a nice, normal job.
4 If I worked in an office, that would be OK.

Grammar

if clauses (revision)

First conditional

1 **Complete the sentences with the correct form of the verbs in brackets.**

1 If my computer crashes again, I .... angry. (be)

2 If you buy Fairtrade products, you .... farmers get a fair price for their goods. (help)

3 If I .... some time this afternoon, I'll go and see that new designer shop in town. (have)

4 I .... that jacket next week if I have enough money. (buy)

5 How .... to school if there's a bus strike tomorrow? (you get)

6 What will I do if I .... you? (lose)

7 Even if she .... me to her party, I won't go. (invite)

8 If she needs anything, she .... you. (phone)

Second conditional

2 **Circle the correct words.**

1 If you *chose / could choose / can choose* to be a famous person for a day, who would it be?

2 If I were you, *I won't / will not / wouldn't* do that.

3 If labour *isn't / wouldn't be / wasn't* so cheap in some countries, the things we buy would be more expensive.

4 Would your parents be angry if you *came / come / will come* home late?

5 *I will / would / would be* buy that car if I had enough money.

6 If I *ask / would ask / asked* the teacher, she might help me.

3 **Look again at the sentences in exercise 2. What are they about?**

1 Possible (but improbable) future situations ☐

2 Impossible situations ☐

4 **Write sentences using the second conditional.**

1 If I / have / a holiday tomorrow / I / stay in bed all day /.

....

2 If I / have / my own plane / I / go on a trip around the world /.

....

3 If I / can / move / to another country / I / go to Australia /.

....

4 If I / get / a sports car for my birthday / I / take you for a drive /.

....

5 If I / can / drive / I / not take the bus /.

....

Grammar

Third conditional

5 Complete the story with the verbs below.

hadn't finished	wouldn't have finished	wouldn't have fallen
hadn't started	hadn't passed	wouldn't have got
wouldn't have moved	hadn't moved	hadn't met wouldn't have met

1 If I .... my exams,
I .... university.

2 If I .... university,
I .... a job at the
bank.

3 If I ....
working at the bank,
I .... to London.

4 If I .... to London, I ....
John.

5 And if I .... John, we ....
in love.

6 Complete the third conditional sentences with the correct form of the verbs in brackets.

1 If you .... (wake) up earlier this morning, you .... (not be) late.

2 I .... (not buy) this computer if .... (know) it was broken.

3 I .... (speak) to him earlier if I .... (knew) he was here.

4 My parents .... (go) to university if they .... (have) the chance.

5 What would you .... (do) if you .... (not pass) your exams?

Skills

Reading

1 Read the article quickly and tick (✓) the best title for it.

1 How Fairtrade has improved our lives ☐

2 How Fairtrade has made our lives worse ☐

3 Why we would never choose Fairtrade coffee ☐

COCOA FARMER KWAME AGYEMAN AND HIS FAMILY TALK ABOUT THE CHANGES FAIRTRADE HAS MADE TO LIVES IN THEIR COMMUNITY.

KWAME AGYEMAN

In this region of Ghana, we depend on the money we get from cocoa to pay for everything we need: food, clothes, school fees and medicine. But in the past, what we got paid was never reliable. Sometimes we didn't get paid at all. Now, the coffee company we work for pays all the farmers a fair price for their cocoa beans, and they pay on time, and in cash. Even if the price of cocoa beans drops, we will still get a secure income.

LINDI AGYEMAN

If it wasn't for Fairtrade policies, I wouldn't be able to send my children to school. When my mother was sick, I had money to send her to the clinic. Fairtrade has literally saved her life – and has made life better for all of us. In our village we have used the extra money that Fairtrade has brought us to build new wells for storing water. Without this, we would have continued to walk for miles every day to collect water from the river. The water was often dirty and made us ill. If we didn't have these wells, many lives would be lost from disease.

KOLI AGYEMAN

I'm very happy that we have this well. This is the first time our village has had clean water. If we sold more of our cocoa beans to Fairtrade companies, we would be able to improve our village facilities even more.

---

2 Read the article again and circle the correct answers.

1 How were workers paid in the past?

   A in cash   **B** irregularly

2 How are workers paid?

   A in cash   **B** by cheque

3 What happens to workers' income if the price of cocoa beans drops?

   A They don't get paid.   **B** They get paid the same.

4 How was Lindi able to help her mother when she got sick?

   A Her mother was able to drink fresh water.   **B** She was able to pay for her to go to the clinic.

5 What would happen if there wasn't fresh water in these villages?

   A More people would die of diseases.   **B** Villagers would have to leave their homes.

Skills

Listening

3 Read the quiz below. What do you think the answers are?

1 How many children around the world don't go to school at the moment?

10 million	40 million	80 million

2 How many adults in the world are unable to read or write?

77 million	717 million	771 million

3 If girls all over the world were educated, just like boys, how many lives would have been saved in the past year?

100,000	1 million	100 million

4 If we want to provide education for all, how many more teachers will we need?

150,000	15 million	1.5 million

50 4 Now listen and check.

51 5 Listen again and complete the information below.

[1] .... million children around the world are currently not in education, mostly [2] .... There are at least [3] .... illiterate adults in the world. At least [4] .... per cent are [5] .... In some countries, like Burkina Faso and Niger, only one in [6] .... girls goes to school. If girls were educated like boys, [7] .... lives would have been saved in the last year. This is because educated [8] .... are in a better position to improve their own health and the health of their families. There is a shortage of [9] .... teachers to provide a good education for boys and girls around the world. If girls were educated to the same level as boys, this would also help make a country more profitable.

Writing

6 Think about something that has made your life better. Choose from the ideas below or use your own ideas. Then make notes on questions 1–3.

someone you met	a job you did	a hobby or sport you started
an exam you passed	something you studied	something you bought

1 Why has it made your life better?
2 How would your life be different if this thing had not happened?
3 If someone wanted to do the same as you, what would you say to them?

7 Write a paragraph about what happened to you.

Planning before you listen

As with reading, when we listen to something, we don't have to understand everything we hear. Unfortunately, listening can be more difficult than reading because we can't make someone speak more slowly, and we can't go back and listen again to something.

Tips

When you listen to something, you should try to do these things.

- Have a good idea **why** you are listening before you start. Are you listening for information? What kind of information?
- Before you listen, predict what the speaker is going to talk about. Try to imagine the words the speaker will use.
- If you hear a word or phrase you don't understand, don't worry too much. It might not be important!

 1 Look at the email below. Try to predict the kind of information missing from each gap. What information do you think you need to listen for?

1 sports and health   2 times, places, money and activities   3 people

---

Re: Caldicot town gym

Hello Sam,

It was great to talk to you about joining the gym. We are always very happy to have new members. I'll just go over the main information here. We are open every day except [1] .... You can come between 6 o'clock in the morning and [2] .... at night.

If you are coming by bike, then there is a bike path by the [3] .... which you can use to get here. You get here in about 20 minutes from the town centre.

If you would like to join our gym, then you can get a [4] .... % discount if you join this [5] ....

We have some great classes. If you want to learn [6] .... or aerobics, then we have some excellent teachers.

Please get in touch if you have any more questions.

All the best,

Amanda Grey (manager)

 2 Now listen to the phone call and complete the email.

3 The two speakers mentioned something about personal trainers and a café. Did you need to understand this to complete the email?

Exam skills 6

Listening

  1 Listen and complete this email with a word or a number in each gap.

Tip Remember to spend time predicting the answers before you listen.

Job interview

Dear Tom,

Thank you very much for writing to us about part-time weekend work. We would like to meet you for a short interview, if that's OK, on ¹ .... 12th February. We would like to start the interview at 9 am but please be at our reception desk at ² ....

Please come to 49 ³ .... Street. You'll find us on the 2nd floor.

You should bring a form of identification, for example a ⁴ .... or a driving licence.

The interview will take about ⁵ .... minutes.

Please tell us before ⁶ .... if you will be able to come.

We look forward to seeing you,

S. Drummer.

  2 Listen again and check your answers.

Writing

3 You receive this email from Tom. What help does he want from you?

Hello!

Can you help me? I've got a job interview next week. Good news, but it means that I have to buy some new clothes. I have no idea where to buy a new suit and a tie. Can you come with me?

Thanks,

Tom

4 Write an email to Tom. Follow the instructions below.

- Congratulate him on his job interview.
- Say that you would like to help him.
- Suggest a time and a place to meet in the town centre.
- Check your email when you finish for any mistakes.

Grammar Review

Present simple Unit 1

The Present simple tense is used for habits and routines, and to talk about facts.
I / You / We / They play football every Saturday.
The match starts at nine o'clock.
I don't eat meat.
My brother doesn't drive.

Present continuous Unit 1

The Present continuous tense is formed with the **Present simple** form of **to be** + infinitive + **-ing**. The **-ing** form is the same for all persons, singular or plural.
I'm having lunch at the moment.
We're watching a DVD.
They aren't studying.
He isn't listening to music. He's talking on his phone.

The Present continuous is used to talk about actions that are in progress at the time of speaking.

Present perfect Unit 1

The Present perfect tense is formed with the **Present** tense of **have** + **past participle**:
They have finished their work.
I have seen the film.

The Past participle of regular verbs is formed like the Past simple by adding **-ed** to the infinitive of the verb.

The Present perfect is used for past actions whose time is not specified.
Ben has left school. He's gone to China for a year.

The Present perfect can be used with **ever** in an interrogative clause and with **never** in a negative clause:
***Have** you **ever skied**?*
*No, I've **never skied**.*

The Present perfect can also express an action beginning in the past which is still continuing. It is often used with **for** (meaning a duration) or **since** (meaning the point in time when the action began):
*I've studied English **for** three years / **since** I was eleven.*

Past continuous Unit 2

The Past continuous tense is formed with the **Past** tense of **to be** + infinitive + **-ing**:
What were you doing last night?
Paula was doing her homework, and I was playing a computer game.

The Past continuous is often used with the Past simple, to show that one action was in progress at a time in the past, when another completed action (in the Past simple) occurred.
I was having a shower when the phone rang.

It is also used with **while** or **as** to show that two actions in the past were happening at the same time.
While *I was waiting for the bus, I was listening to music on my MP3 player.*
*I was thinking about the holidays **as** I was lying in bed.*

Past perfect Unit 2

The Past perfect tense is formed with the **Past** tense of **have** + **past participle**:
He hadn't been at school for a few days, because he'd been ill.

The Past perfect is used to show that one action in the past happened before another.
When I got to the concert, the band had started to play.
I had just finished my breakfast when I heard the doorbell ring.

should / shouldn't and ought / oughtn't Unit 3

Should and *shouldn't* are used to say what we think is a good idea, and to give advice. They are followed by the infinitive of the verb.
You should buy things online – it's much easier.
You shouldn't tell anyone your bank details.

We can also use *ought to* + the infinitive of the verb. The negative – *ought not (oughtn't)* – is not used very often.

Gerunds Unit 3

A Gerund is the **-ing** form of a verb. It can be used as the subject or as the object of a verb.
Shopping *is my favourite hobby!* (subject)
*I like **swimming** and **playing** tennis.* (object)

Grammar Review

Talking about the future Unit 4

Be going to/ Present continuous

We use **be going to** + infinitive to talk about future intentions.
I'm going to study drama when I leave school.
What are you going to do when you arrive in Paris?
Shannon's going to design her own dress for the party.

The Present continuous is also used to talk about the future. We usually use it to talk about fixed arrangements for the future.
I've got a holiday job for the summer. I'm working in a shop.
We're having a barbeque on the beach on Saturday.

Future time clauses Unit 4

As soon as, ***when***, ***before*** and ***after*** are often used to talk about actions in the future. In these phrases, the verb is in the present tense:
Please knock on the door before you come into the room.
I'll phone you as soon as I get home.
When I leave school, I'm going to travel for a year.
Let's go for a coffee after the lesson ends.

so / such Unit 5

We can use **such** before a noun and **so** before an adjective to emphasise the quality of the noun or adjective. We can also talk about the result by adding *that* followed by a clause.
*It was **such** a nice day that we decided to have a picnic in the park.*
*I was **so** hot that I jumped straight into the water.*
*I'd never been into **such** a wonderful building before.*
*I was **so** tired after the trip to the theme park.*

Phrasal verbs Unit 5

Verbs followed by a preposition which cannot immediately be understood by looking at the individual words, are called phrasal verbs. The meaning of the verb often changes depending on the preposition following it:
take after = be similar to; **take up** = start a new hobby or activity;
turn up = increase the volume; **turn into** = become;
turn off = use a switch to stop a radio, etc. from operating

The passive

Unit 6

The Present simple passive has the following structure:
Subject + **Present simple** of **be** (not) + **Past participle**.

French is taught in most schools in the U.K.

The Past simple passive has the following structure:

Subject + **Past simple** of **be** (not) + **Past participle**.

The festival was held in June, on the Isle of Wight.

make / let / be allowed to

Unit 6

Make + **object** + **infinitive** without 'to' expresses obligation:
*She **made** the teacher very cross when she didn't listen.*
Let + **object** + **infinitive** without 'to' is used to express permission to do a certain action:
My parents don't let me listen to music while I do my homework.

The passive form of *let* is the verb **to be** + **(past participle) allowed**. The past participle is the same for all persons, singular and plural.
Are you allowed to stay out later than midnight?
Fran isn't allowed to wear make-up.
We aren't allowed to use mobile phones at school.

will / won't

Unit 7

When we are sure about something in the future, we can use **will** (='ll) or **won't** (= will not) plus the infinitive of the verb.
There'll be food and drink at the party.
I won't be late.
Will you come?

Question tags

Unit 7

Question tags are short phrases added to the end of a sentence to ask for agreement.
An affirmative sentence is followed by a negative question tag; a negative sentence is followed by a positive question tag.
He likes swimming, doesn't he?
You've met Tom before, haven't you?
They aren't English, are they?
She didn't go to the party, did she?

Grammar Review

could, might, may for speculation
Unit 8

We can use **could**, **might** and **may** to talk about possible situations and hypothesise about a situation. As always, these modal verbs are followed by the infinitive without *to*.
Jo may study German next year.
The bus could arrive any time between 5 p.m. and 6 p.m.
I might go to the concert tonight – I'm not sure.

-ed vs -ing adjectives
Unit 8

Some adjectives have two forms: *bored/boring, confused/confusing, surprised/surprising* etc. Generally we use the **-ed** adjective to describe the feeling we have.
I'm confused. (= I don't understand something.)

We use the **-ing** adjective to describe the thing that produces that feeling.
The work was confusing. (= It made me feel confused.)

used to
Unit 9

Used to (**didn't use to**) expresses a past routine:
*We **used to** go to the Youth Club on Fridays, but we don't any more.*
*We **didn't use to** have a dog, but now we have got one.*

The interrogative form **did … use to?** is rarely used.

Gerunds after prepositions
Unit 9

Many verbs and adjectives are followed by a preposition. If we want to use a verb after the preposition, the verb is in the **-ing** form.

Our teacher insists on speaking only English in class.
I'm not very good at running.
Is Jeremy interested in learning judo?

Present perfect continuous
Unit 10

The Present perfect continuous tense is formed with the **person** + **have** + **been** + **-ing** form of the verb:

Something smells nice in the kitchen. Have you been baking?
Yes, I've been baking bread.

The Present perfect continuous is used to show that something has been in progress for a certain period, up to the moment of speaking and is still going on.

Embedded questions

Embedded questions are questions that are hidden in a sentence.
They often begin with *I don't know ......, Nobody knows ......, I have no idea. ......* etc.
The question word follows the expressions above:
*When does he arrive? = I don't know **when** he arrives.*
*How do you do this sum? = Nobody knows **how** to do this sum.*

Reported speech

Reported speech is a construction used to relate someone's opinion, message or statement, without necessarily using the speaker's exact words. Reported speech is usually introduced by the verbs **say** and **tell**. **Say** can be followed by **that** but not by an object.
*She **says (that)** she wants a drink.*

Tell is usually followed by an object pronoun and can then be followed by **that**.
*Sam **tells me (that)** he is in the drama club.*

When reported speech is introduced by **say** or by **tell** in the Present tense there are no changes. The tenses are the same as in the direct speech:
'I am writing a test.' He **says (tells me)** that he's writing a test.*

If reported speech is introduced by **say** or **tell** in the Past, tenses change as follows:
Present simple > Past simple
'I am going home.' She said that she was going home.*
Present continuous > Past continuous
'We're leaving in five minutes.' They said that they were leaving in five minutes.*
Past simple > Past perfect
'You didn't do the work.' The teacher said that I hadn't done the work.*
Present perfect > Past perfect
'I've been to the library already.' She said she'd been to the library already.*
Will > Would
'I will see you tomorrow.' He said that he would see me the next day.*

N.B Some subject pronouns in direct speech change as follows in reported speech:
I > he / she
you (singular) **> I**
you (plural) **> we**
we > they

Grammar Review

Reported questions

When we report a question, we use verbs like **ask**, **wonder** and **want to know**. Tense changes are the same as for reported speech (see p. 79).
If the question has a question word like **when/how/why** we use the same question word in the reported question.
'When is Janet coming?' He **asked** *me when Janet was coming.*

If the question doesn't have a question word, we use the word **if** or **whether** in the reported question.
'Can I sit here?' I **wondered** *if I could sit there.*
'Will you help me?' She **wanted to know** *whether/if I would help her.*

*If-*clauses

Use the **first conditional** to talk about things that are possible or likely to happen in the future.
The first conditional is formed with the *If-*clause:
If + subject + Present simple + Main clause: subject + ***will/won't*** + infinitive.
If I get home early enough, I'll phone you.

We use the **second conditional** to talk about situations that we don't expect to happen. The second conditional is formed with the *If-*clause:
If + subject + Past simple + Main clause: subject + ***would/wouldn't*** + infinitive.
If I found a nice second-hand jacket, I'd buy it.

To ask a question using the first or second conditional you simply reverse the word order.
Will you phone me if you get home early enough?
Would you buy a second-hand jacket if you found a nice one?